Letter To Bob Avakian

Letter to Bob Avakian

by Caleb Maupin

Copyright © 2023 by Caleb Maupin

⊕ Center for Political Innovation
Dedicated to educating and fostering visions for a future beyond capitalism

All rights reserved. No part of this publication may be reproduced, stored in a retrieval system, or transmitted, in any form or by any means, electronic, mechanical, photocopying, recording, or otherwise, without the prior written permission of Caleb Maupin.

Table of Contents

1. You deserve more respect 1
2. An aspect of your strength 13
3. Idealism vs. Materialism 35
4. How Can We Achieve The Higher Stage of Communism? 51
5. What Makes A Country Socialist? 60
6. The Anti-Imperialist World Today 72
7. Jacobinism not Marxism 92
8. The label of "economism" 104
9. Imperialism is a system 113
10. Russia and China are NOT imperialists 124
12. Divisions in the ruling class, strategic alliances 142
13. The Boston Trap 163
14. They used you in 1979 181
15. French Imperialism & Covert Manipulation 201
16. Old and New Atheism 225
17. "inspired by their belief in God" 234
18. The God I Found 245
19. "Where Does This Revolution Come From?" 267

You don't get the respect you deserve. It is so easy to criticize from a distance, spout off with loud-mouthed oversimplifications, repeat gossip and slander, to mock from a distance, or feign knowledge. These are things that anybody can do to pad their own ego and write somebody off. But what you have done over the course of your eight decades of life is hard, not easy and you deserve recognition.

1. You deserve more respect

I first considered writing this letter in the aftermath of the U.S. Supreme Court's decision to overturn Roe v. Wade on June 24, 2022. At the time, protests in support of abortion led by the organization "Rise Up For Abortion Rights" were being organized by your comrade Sunsara Taylor. *Yahoo News*, *VICE*, *The Daily Beast* and *The*

Intercept, all decided to pile condemnation onto Sunsara's work despite more or less agreeing with her support for keeping abortion legal. The hit pieces decided to bait Sunsara Taylor for being associated with the Revolutionary Communist Party, the organization you have dedicated your life to building.

My political orientation toward the Supreme Court's move was completely different from yours and Sunsara's. My feeling is that the abortion issue is a trap, a culture war, that serves as a barrier to class unity. Even though I disapproved of some of Sunsara's tactics and disagreed with her rhetoric, as I read the articles piling condemnation onto you and those who you have worked with, I was filled with disgust. The language was toxic but predictable. *The Intercept* quoted so-called "experts" describing a "weird cult" "scam front run by an MLM cult." There were accusations of "social justice front groups" "co-opting social movements." *VICE* quoted talk of "pyramid schemes that prey on social movements." These "progressive" publications were playing on the ignorance of their audience. Anyone who knows anything about you or your organization knows that you have been in the streets, organizing since long before the woke activists of generation Z were ever born. Decades before Twitter, before Facebook, members of the Revolutionary Communist Party were out in the streets talking about unpopular issues like police brutality and racism. If anything, they are the ones co-opting the very language and causes you and your comrades have raised for so long, often in political climates where it was far less trendy and accepted.

The barrage of hate and cancel culture directed toward yourself, Sunsara and the RCP was a total misrepresentation of your years of selfless organizing and heroic sacrifice. They glossed over it all, not interested in the truth but rather in simply finding a "scandal" or "controversy" they could gain social clout for "calling out." Canceling Sunsara and running your organization's name through the mud was a convenient vehicle for getting some attention, especially when "cults" are the obsession of Netflix documentaries, and the propaganda of the woke liberal order battling against Trump.

If they had approached me for comment on the issue, something they would most likely never have done as I have also been canceled for my work with Russian media and have had my own organization labeled a "cult," I would have given them a very different picture of you. If I had been approached as an expert, I would have told them about a young man from Berkeley, California who grew up in relative luxury, as the son of prominent Judge,

Spurgeon Avakian, who even served on the California Supreme Court. I would explain how this young man got involved in activism on his campus demanding the right of students to organize around off-campus issues like civil rights. I would tell how amid the historic events called

In 1976, the Revolutionary Communist Party organized a large protest to counter the bicentennial celebrations in Philadelphia.

"The Free Speech Movement" at UC Berkeley, a young man who had just recovered from a devastating illness became a firebrand political organizer, getting arrested, putting his body on the line and empowering other people to step up.

I would point out how the Black Panther Party, a group of African-Americans who organized armed patrols in nearby Oakland, had attracted you as an ally. How you became one of the most outspoken white supporters of this organization of Black revolutionaries. How you led the Peace and Freedom Party as an electoral entity for the radical movements of the time, helping put Black Panthers and opponents of the Vietnam war on the ballot. I would tell them how you worked with and wrote for *Ramparts* magazine, a cutting edge publication in the Bay Area that gave voice to the anti-war movement and was read across the planet.

I would tell them how you formed an organization called the Revolutionary Union, recruiting people who were engaged in anti-war and anti-racist activism and teaching them Marxist-Leninist ideology. I would tell them how your organization became the Revolutionary Communist Party in 1975, a group which remains one of the biggest and most visible communist groups in the country.

On July 4th, 1976, when the country was celebrating the bi-centennial, your organization organized a protest called "We've Carried The Rich for 200 Years, Now Lets Dump Them Off Our Backs!" Thousands of people marched against U.S. imperialism in the streets of Philadelphia. Among them were many Vietnam veterans, and the photograph of former soldiers in uniform marching behind a banner that says "We Won't

Fight Another Rich Man's War" is beautiful, powerful and iconic.

I would tell them how your organization protested against nuclear escalation with the Soviet Union, organizing "No Business As Usual" protests against President Ronald Reagan's war provocations. I would tell them how "Refuse and Resist" was established to oppose the rising prison industrial complex and police state during the late 1980s. I would tell how your member's played a role in the Los Angeles riots, a rebellion against racism after the horrendous torture of Rodney King in 1992.

Long before police brutality was a trendy issue, I walked shoulder to shoulder with your disciples in the streets of Cleveland to condemn the police killing of Brandon McCloud. Your organization also helped negotiate a gang truce in Los Angeles in the aftermath of the 1992 riots and have been trusted supporters and allies of police brutality victims across the country.

When I first encountered your organization they were involved in opposing the war in Iraq and rallying to "Drive Out The Bush Regime." A crew of 19 and 20-year-olds in Cleveland would come to every anti-war protest with Red Flags, chanting "Not My President! No My War! This whole system is rotten to the core!" Often the chants were followed up with speeches quoting your writings and venerating your leadership.

For decades you have sat at the helm of an organization that has made a massive contribution to the struggle for justice. You have opposed every ugly war the U.S. government has waged and been key organizers of the anti-war protest movements. You have stood up against the police state and political repression, teaming up with the ACLU to fight for freedom of speech and oppose surveillance, taking the struggle to the court rooms. Your organization has taught Marxism and made a point of visibly promoting communism even as mainstream media and academia celebrated "the death of Marxism" and "the end of history."

The Revolutionary Communist Party, though small, still exists. It has bookstores, newspapers, a website, and a visible presence wherever left-wing dissidents are found. Most of the many similar organizations that emerged during the New Communist Movement of the 1970s faded away. The Communist Workers Party is gone. The October League is gone. The Communist Labor Party is gone. The Marxist-Leninist Party is gone. Both *The Guardian* and *Line of March* long ago went out of print. Bob Avakian and the RCP are still alive and kicking. That is a testament to a unique form of strength, and edgy teenagers trying on Marxism as a new outfit and snarking about it on the internet have no idea how difficult it must have been to accomplish this longevity and legacy.

You have made significant personal sacrifices and endured much persecution for your relentlessness. You've spent many nights in jail. You've been beaten up and injured by police. You faced serious criminal charges in Washington DC. You even fled the country and moved to France, fearing for your safety, applying for political exile status in 1982.

Your choice to give your life to what America considers a taboo, forbidden ideology has cost you on a deeply personal level. In your autobiography *From Ike to Mao and Beyond* you spoke of how you were unable to attend the funerals of either of your parents when they died. Amid the political turmoil of decades past you have had many comrades betray you. Your memoir describes how your spouse was harassed. Scathing attacks on your personality, ugly rumors and gossip, all intended to discredit your prowess as a leader have been circulated. You endured all of this and held your organization together, enabling it to do its important work.

The childish responses I often hear from younger communists when your name is mentioned are completely unfair. None of them have made the sacrifices you have made. None of them have held a Communist group together through the turmoil of decades and decades of political confusion and reaction. None of them have made anywhere near the contribution you have made over the years.

Rather than turning their noses up, many people my age and younger should be listening to you. You have a lot to teach us. You have accomplished what many of us could only dream of. You have played an important role in the struggle against imperialism and the struggle for justice in the United States. You have certainly left your mark on the class struggle in America.

2. An aspect of your strength

I have found I gain much more insight by noticing the strengths of political figures I may disagree with or be critical of than simply articulating my differences. As I have watched you from a distance and studied the history of Communist organizations in recent US history, your name and your organization has come up often. As I have looked over your organization, both its contemporary shifts and activities and the historical accounts and primary source materials published on the Marxist Internet Archive, and reflected on my own direct experience of observing your organization in the street, I have gained a particular insight.

What makes your work and the organization you have built unique is a certain blend of burning passion one does not find elsewhere. When I encountered your followers promoting a national day of action to "drive out the Bush regime," they had an excited momentum. They spoke of the upcoming date of protests around the country as "the beginning of the end of the Bush regime" and possibly "determining the fate of the country for decades to come." The members were in a frenzy calling people to raise money, putting up posters, distributing leaflets, staying up late, waking up early, all building up to a national day of action. They took the dangers of the moment quite seriously, and they sincerely believed their activism could make a difference. People quit their jobs, skipped class or even dropped out of school. It was "now or never." The fate of humanity was at stake. It was time to "Go! Go! Go!"

I directly observed how your organization has the ability to create a level of collective energy, excitement, passion, almost mania in the build up to its national actions. The cultivation of this atmosphere, of course, can directly be attributed to you, the man at the top. This ability to create passion and energy enables your organization, despite having views that put them on the fringe the American political spectrum, to be noticed in mainstream media and to impact the political conversation. Your organization runs advertisements in the New York Times, builds massive events at Riverside Church featuring yourself alongside Dr. Cornel West, convenes massive political mobilizations opposing Donald Trump or police brutality. The energy you create around these mobilizations is so strong that many people who are not ready to become Communists or join your organization get caught in the passion as well. They feel the momentum created by the RCP's latest drive to change the political conversation and they are attracted to it. The RCP is not a talk shop, a debating society, but an organization of action, and this action creates a gravity that pulls people around it consistently.

As I remember the atmosphere created around the "Drive Out The Bush Regime" national days of action I participated in as a college-aged radical, and then look over the history of your organization, it all makes sense to me.

I recall talking to older Communists from different corners of the country who described reading your call to support the Richmond Oil Workers against Standard Oil Company in *The Guardian*, and packing up and heading to California. In the atmosphere of 1969, with a political upsurge among college radicals, you called on students to go support the picket lines and "combine the student movement with the labor movement." An article describing the events reports of "a large number of students from different groups and backgrounds, walking the picket lines and as well as a strategy-level alliance between local union officials and leaders of the Revolutionary Union."

The article describes how "One night a company goon squad beat up a couple of pickets with chains. The next night a mass mobilization was held to wipe out the goon squad. We gathered at the union hall, over a hundred of us, the workers in hard hats, the students in campus riot gear…" The article criticizes the student radicals you mobilized for "putting themselves in place of the workers" but the account provided of the events is no less inspiring. The article says: "A typical incident went something like this: Four or five union men plus fifteen or twenty students marching in a circle in front of the gate. A company car or truck pulls up and tries to crash the picket line. Several students smash the car's windows with rocks and sticks... after one of these episodes I

The "May Day 1980" campaign mobilized thousands of people to take to the streets in the name of Communism.

heard a middle aged worker say "Boy, these students really mean business!"

Of course they did! With your charismatic leadership and brilliance you inspired them to come to Richmond California from the East Coast, the South, and the Midwest. You pointed out that student radicalism was not enough and that the involvement of the working class was needed to make a revolution. You created an atmosphere of "the time is now!" and brought them into the struggle. Hundreds of young Communists went to Richmond to join the picket lines because you called them, you convinced them it needed to be done, and you inspired them to take action.

When I read accounts of the founding conventions of the youth activist group you created, the Attica Brigade, I get this same brilliant energy. When I read accounts of the May Day 1980 mobilizations your organization called a decade later, the same energy glows through each word. In January of 1980, your organization put out a call to build May Day Brigades: "The Revolutionary Communist Party is issuing a call to those who urgently see the need to wake up our broader ranks to volunteer to join Revolutionary May Day Brigades. These brigades will travel to key battle areas, spreading experiences and heightening this fight as a nationwide effort of our class. The storm around May Day will be built mainly through local efforts in the industrial and urban centers of this country, and the major cities where workers and others will march on May 1. May Day will be built in these cities by drawing forward and activating new revolutionary-minded workers in a way never seen before in this country… These brigades will be traveling for the three months from now right up to when May Day will occur, striking with lightning force to electrify the scene…Just imagine:

Brigades of fighters from the working class of all nationalities, native and foreign-born, students and others who enthusiastically see the potential for May Day 1980, converging together on cities and also hitting other areas of capitalism's powers; challenging their class brothers and sisters to actually march May 1 in their true revolutionary interests and join the ranks of the international proletariat; miners from the hills of West Virginia; brigades of auto and steel workers; workers from the garment sweatshops that rot in the shadows of New York skyscrapers… We're calling on workers and others to make the sacrifice of leaving home and family to carry the message to distant neighborhoods, factories, mills and unemployment offices–living proof of the strength our class has when we're unleashed, a potential that will burst loose on a grand scale on May Day 1980."

Hundreds of people responded to your call, and spent months mobilizing for May Day 1980. Your press reported on how your small organization was able to electrify the country with energy: "May Day was everywhere. An editorial letter submitted to a Cleveland paper complaining about taxes ended with, "is it any wonder that those of us with poor-paying jobs are so ready to join the May Day Revolutionary Brigade?" It had become a reference point. Even in the heart of one of their military training camps–Fort Lewis, near Tacoma, Washington–army brass walked out one morning to find GI's had covered the walls of a lifesize German town training replica with May Day posters. The same kind of thing was occurring among American GI's stationed in West Germany. Revolution was being discussed and argued on a scale unseen in years, it began to be seized on by the advanced as the realizable alternative. "We

Won't Work That Day–Will You?"–the idea captured the imagination of millions, and many were weighing the question seriously. People, especially workers, began to go through soul searching and intense ideological struggle with themselves. A young worker in a plant where several others in his department were taking up May Day said, "I feel like the man in the poster, I want to step out but what can one person do?"....In just the three months leading up to and including May 1st, 800 were arrested, over $500.000 was paid in bail, many were held in jail for weeks for ransom. From the beginning the hand of the highest authorities could be seen behind this onslaught of attacks....Millions were watching, anticipating. Thousands lined the streets, some with homemade red flags, others with eggs and bottles. Riot cops were everywhere. Throughout the day many radio programs gave updated reports on the battles in the streets of the target cities–New York, Washington D.C., Atlanta, Chicago, Detroit, Oakland, Los Angeles–as well as nine other cities across the country. In Portland, a Black worker speaking before the march began looked straight out at a crowd of idiots that had come wearing "Fuck You-Iran" t-shirts and said to them, "This is International Workers Day. This march isn't going to be stopped by guys like you or anybody else." An older white worker, a Korean vet and prisoner of war, jumped into the march in D.C... "Some guys on the corner were talking about stopping you guys. I told them they'd have to go through me first. What I learned from the POW camp and when I came back was that my enemy was right here. I learned that freedom has got to be fought for, it doesn't come bloodless." A woman in Oakland saw the red flags coming down the street. She remembered this was International Workers

Day, grabbed her kid and fought her way through cop barricades to finally join up. Two taxicabs filled with eight Latino workers pulled over in downtown Los Angeles and jumped out and into the march. Other forces lent their support in the battle–clergy in Oakland formed a contingent to "prevent a police riot," students from Iran, the Middle East, Ethiopia and more joined in...The bourgeoisie claimed that May 1 was an insignificant and lost battle. Their newscasts focused on a carefully constructed portrait of "crazed violence." But the news of this "insignificant event" was carried all day and into the next and ran on the front page of many, many papers. Several weeks later one of their own DJ's opened a radio show saying he had two things to discuss, "The first, May Day and the RCP you already know about. You heard it on the 5 o'clock news, the 6 o'clock, 7, 10, 11 o'clock news . . " And weeks later when covering RCP trials in San Francisco, as workers and others sang the Internationale, a news commentator described the day's events as "familiar scenes." Clearly May Day penetrated into most every nook and cranny of political life in this country."

What I observe in your history as a leader is a factor that tells a lot about the history of the Communist movement. It makes me think about Anna Louise Strong and her book *The Stalin Era,* which describes the atmosphere of construction and optimism that industrialized the Soviet Union with the 5-year-plans. It makes me think of Edgar Snow's writings about Mao Zedong and the Eighth Route Army. Young Chinese people from across the country left their old lives behind, came to the Red Army camp, adopted a new name and new identity and selflessly gave themselves to the battle for creating a new China.

It was not uncommon for writers such as Agnes Smedley or William Hinton to compare the atmosphere of Mao's movement in 1930s China to early Christianity. I think this comparison is probably absolutely correct, but what it points to is in contrast to the hard materialism and economic determinism one finds among Marxists.

The role of individuals like yourself as charismatic leaders, filled with passion, urging people to be bolder, stronger, and more dedicated, to work harder and fight with passion, to live selflessly and give themselves to the future was a very important aspect of 20th Century socialism. Stalin was the first such figure, but the political and economic model he pioneered was adopted in China, Cuba, Eastern Europe and Vietnam, and many other corners of the planet. In an almost entirely state-run economy undergoing rapid industrialization with 5-year-plans, collectivized agriculture, and single-ruling ideological party, the role of a highly charismatic leader incarnating the national project of rising up is essential. What Khruschev later denounced as "cult of personality" has a spiritual quality. It was an essential part of the mobilizations to raise countries up from poverty under the leadership of Marxist-Leninist parties. Many countries around the world were transformed by an economic model of development that relied on such a figure, who had the ability to pull out the best from people and empower them to do amazing things.

Though this aspect of 20th Century "really existing socialism" is unacknowledged in Marxist economic textbooks, you applied it to building and leading your small political sect in the United States of America. You learned the method of motivating people to build, bonding people together with a common mission, and creating an atmosphere of anticipation for the upcoming national day of action. This method you developed held your organization together decade after decade, and gave it the strength to force itself to be acknowledged and relevant in political discourse, as small and "fringe" as it may be.

You have been attacked for allegedly stating you sought to build a "cult of personality" around yourself. Those who level this attack against you fail to realize that to whatever degree you achieved this, it has a lot to do with the success and endurance of your organization over the years. Many people attached themselves to your teachings and your political mission and gained validation for themselves by putting it into practice. Other organizations that failed to create the same kind of passionate, emotional and dedicated atmosphere faded away. The Revolutionary Communist Party remains.

The ideology of liberalism glorifies the individual above all else. It celebrates "thinking for yourself" and views any kind of group cohesion or collectivism with contempt. "Communists" and socialists in America are largely infected with this kind of thinking. For them socialism is a way to appear "edgy," to rebel and define themselves in opposition to the anti-communist society they live in. However, I attribute the limited success your organization has had over the years and your organization's survival over the years of decline as other communist groups collapsed, largely to your *illiberalism*. To some degree or other your organization mimics the non-liberal and non-individualistic thinking of the foreign Communist movements it takes inspiration from.

I do not think there is something fundamentally wrong with you presenting yourself as "the leader of the revolution." I do not think there is anything fundamentally wrong with your organization seeking to build a "culture of appreciation" for your teachings and work. I may have criticism of how this has been carried out, and I certainly have massive criticism of your work and perspective, but the liberal disgust for charismatic leadership and group mobilization is a toxic aspect of our decaying western culture.

Human beings are naturally collective creatures. Since the dawn of time, they have organized themselves into groups, and these groups have almost always had an individual who plays the executive role. Every country has a head of state. Every corporation has a CEO. Every workplace has a manager. Every classroom has a teacher. I reject the notion that leaders are bad or that idealizing a political thinker or philosopher, or having a charismatic individual as the face of a political movement is dangerous authoritarianism.

This is a brain-worm, a mind infection, planted by liberals during the cold war and leading to so much utter demoralization in our time.

Sure, as Communists, we seek an egalitarian society without a state and without coercion. We seek to dismantle all social hierarchies in the long term. But I can imagine that even in the ideal Communist world, some kind of leadership will exist, as non-coercive, voluntary and egalitarian as it may be. In my experience, even the most "free thinking" and cynical people have a celebrity, public figure, or artist that they idealize, even if privately. The liberal opposition to the very concept of hero-worship runs contrary to the way human societies tend to function.

In an entity that has effectively carried out many political operations over the years and remained intact despite the climate dramatically changing, you played an essential role. You as the "man at the top," the leader, the public face, are like CEOs at an effective start-up company. Perhaps one can think of how Napoleon's detractors called him the "one hundred thousand man" because with his energy and passion, he propelled a massive army.

The task you took on for yourself was attempted by many would-be chairman and aspiring American Lenins among the baby boomer generation. Most of them gave up after a decade at most. Names like Mike Klonsky, Micheal Laski, Jerry Tung, Marlene Dixon, and Clayton Van Lydegraf have faded from most people's memories. They were unable to accomplish anything near what you have done in the last 50 years. Despite all the mud thrown at you and all the posturing and petty criticism directed at you, you have had far more success at carrying out a highly difficult task.

Perhaps by your own standards, none of this matters. Your organization fixates on the slogan *Revolution, Nothing Less*. But I think short of seizing power in a revolution you have indeed accomplished a lot. Your organization is one of the main reasons Mumia Abu Jamal is still alive and breathing. Your organization got flag burning legalized by the U.S. Supreme Court and stimulated years of debate about compulsory patriotism and freedom of speech. Your organization built huge protests, calling out the ugly wars US imperialism has waged. I have seen with my own eyes that your organization gave critical support to the surviving family members of those murdered by the police and supported them consistently for decades.

None of this is irrelevant. None of this can be discounted, and none of it would be possible if you, as the man at the top and the lightning rod of personal attacks and threats of repression, did not indeed possess serious skills as a leader and motivator of your comrades.

3. Idealism vs. Materialism

Marxism as an ideology places itself solidly in the camp of materialists and against idealism; a debate which goes back to ancient Greek philosophers. Does the mind create reality or does reality create the mind? The idealist Descartes said "I think, therefore, I am." The dialectical materialist Friedrich Engels said "Thought is inseparable from matter that thinks."

Marx's materialism was unlike that of previous materialist philosophers, in that he not only argued that matter was all that existed and rejected the existence of any spiritual plane or supernatural energy. Marx argued that the matter that existed was "dialectical" and in a constant state of conflict and change. This view of the world as being nothing but solid existence, but this solid existence never being static and constantly evolving and changing due to clashes and contradictions is called Dialectical Materialism.

I admit that despite considering Marxism-Leninism and the Global Communist Movement to be a big part of my ideological heritage, I have broken with the purely dialectical materialist worldview. I believe in the existence of God, though not in the same sense as others. I also believe in the power of ideas, the power of the human will, the power of love and intention in altering the nature of reality.

I admit I am not a pure materialist, but I will argue that neither are you. I see idealism not merely in the manner in which you mobilize your followers to selflessly devote themselves to political mobilizations. I see idealism in many of your stated beliefs and writings.

For an organization that presents itself as Marxist and specifically emphasizes atheism and materialism, I see very little interest in economics. Marx's understanding of the irrationality of capitalism is highly relevant in our time. Labor is being replaced by machines at a level previously unheard of with Artificial Intelligence. Marx's concepts about the worker's competition with machines, the tendency of the falling rate of profit, the problem of overproduction, are all highly important and need to be widely understood. The built-in problems of a system where human beings only value is their ability to create surplus value for an employer, a system where the means of production only function in order to maximize profit for their owners are back with a vengeance.

Yet, in the publications of the Revolutionary Communist Party and in your writings, I do not find articles bemoaning poverty amid plenty, explaining the root of the economic crisis in the tech revolution, calling for the working class to mobilize in its own economic interests in order to seize the means of production. Instead I hear condemnations of Republicans as being racist and fascist. I hear endless talk of achieving "a world without oppression, exploitation, poverty and destruction of the environment" and "a whole different way to organize society, a whole better world, is possible."

The economic problems of capitalism are not bemoaned and the vision of socialism that is put forward is not one where the fundamental irrationality of production for profit is eliminated. When I open the pages *Basics* or listen to speeches such as *Revolution: Nothing Less* or *Revolution:*

Why its Possible, Why its Necessary and What its All About, I hear articulated the ugly history of lynching and Jim Crow segregation. I hear articulated outrage about police brutality and the violent nature of the U.S. state apparatus. I find a crass rejection and lampooning of the jingoism and patriotism that was once much more common in U.S. society. All of this is admirable and correct. But it is also something that any MSNBC liberal or woke social media personality could say as well.

You must admit that your proclamation that "there wouldn't be a U.S. Imperialism in the way there is today if it weren't for the exploitation of Black people under slavery" and your call on people to "conceive of a world without America – without everything America stands for and everything it does in the world" could have been written by the 1619 Project of *The New York Times.*

In the age of woke politics, there's no longer anything edgy or radical about saying you are triggered by the American flag or condemning police brutality in rhetoric laced with profanity. It is good that police brutality and racial inequality is widely acknowledged in ways it previously has not been. However, white guilt radicalism and campus SJW virtue signaling are everywhere in US society these days, and much of it has very little to do with anything Karl Marx wrote about.

Though you allude to class relations, empowering the masses of people, a new economic system, your rhetoric sounds very similar to that of modern day woke moralists. Your critique of US society seems to be that there are bad people who are selfish, racist, chauvinistic and cruel who run the state. Your solution, laid out in your Constitution for the New Socialist America and your calls on your audience to "imagine" a new society, emphasize solving this problem by "taking power" and putting moral people in their place to rule according to a more ethical and rational worldview.

Karl Marx's philosophy is rooted in dialectical and historical materialism, rejecting idealism.

This is idealism, not materialism. The current order is directed by bad ideas (racism, sexism, religious superstition, chauvinism) and it is to be resolved by imposing good ideas (anti-racism, science, atheism). This misses the very essence of everything Marx wrote about. Marx did not speak of good people with good ideas battling bad people with bad ideas. He spoke of economic classes, struggling for power out of material interest, pushing humanity to advance toward higher modes of production.

In the statement "We Are the Revcoms" found on your website, your organization describes its activities this way: "Basing ourselves on the scientific method of the new communism, we actively apply the strategic approach of Fight the Power, and Transform the People, for Revolution: involving masses of people in rising up to resist the continuing crimes of this system, and defending people from attacks on their rights and their lives by racist, woman-hating and anti-LGBTQ thugs, in and out of government... winning people to the scientific understanding that *we do not have to live this way*—that this system of capitalism-imperialism is the root cause and fundamental source of all the unnecessary suffering that masses of people are subjected to, here and throughout the world, and poses a growing threat to the very existence of humanity through the accelerating destruction of the environment and increasing danger of nuclear war—<u>and</u> that *we need to, and can, bring a whole different and much better system and world into being through revolution...* In this way, we are working to carry out the **three prepares**: *prepare the ground* (the necessary conditions for revolution); *prepare the people*, in the millions, for this revolution; and *prepare the leadership*, in the thousands, based on the new communism, that is necessary in order for this revolution to succeed."

Such stated goals are not exactly off the mark, but what does this really involve and mean? Joining Black Lives Matter protests? Echoing CNN and MSNBC in calling Trump a Nazi? Condemning America for being a "racist" country? Popularizing a prematurely written constitution for a new socialist republic? In practice, this certainly summarizes your organization's work in recent years and in the end it consists of spreading your ideas, pushing forward your own concepts of morality in opposition to those of others and arguing that you are more fit to rule on the basis of your more rational and moral stances. This idealism, not materialism.

Let's contrast this with what is written in the Communist Manifesto. This is how Marx describes the working class becoming politicized and moving to take power: "But with the development of industry, the proletariat not only increases in number; it becomes concentrated in greater masses, its strength grows, and it feels that strength more. The various interests and conditions of life within the ranks of the proletariat are more and more equalized, in proportion as machinery obliterates all distinctions of labor, and nearly everywhere reduces wages to the same low level. The growing competition among the bourgeois, and the resulting commercial crises, make the wages of the workers ever more fluctuating. The increasing improvement of machinery, ever more rapidly developing, makes their livelihood more and more precarious; the collisions between individual workmen and individual bourgeois take more and more the character of collisions between two classes. **Thereupon, the workers begin to form combinations against the bourgeois; they**

club together in order to keep up the rate of wages; they found permanent associations in order to make provision beforehand for these occasional revolts. Here and there, the contest breaks out into riots. Now and then the workers are victorious, but only for a time. **The real fruit of their battles lies, not in the immediate result, but in the ever expanding union of the workers.** This union is helped on by the improved means of communication that are created by modern industry, and that place the workers of different localities in contact with one another. It was just this contact that was needed to centralize the numerous local struggles, all of the same character, into one national struggle between classes. But every class struggle is a political struggle… **This organization of the proletarians into a class, and, consequently into a political party, is continually being upset again by the competition between**

LETTER TO BOB AVAKIAN

the workers themselves. But it ever rises up again, stronger, firmer, mightier. It compels legislative recognition of particular interests of the workers, by taking advantage of the divisions among the bourgeoisie itself. Thus, the ten-hours' bill in England was carried. Altogether collisions between the classes of the old society further, in many ways, the course of development of the proletariat. The bourgeoisie finds itself involved in a constant battle. At first with the aristocracy; later on, with those portions of the bourgeoisie itself, whose interests have become antagonistic to the progress of industry; at all time with the bourgeoisie of foreign countries. In all these battles, it sees itself compelled to appeal to the proletariat, to ask for help, and thus, to drag it into the political arena. **The bourgeoisie itself, therefore, supplies the proletariat with its own elements of political and general education, in**

other words, it furnishes the proletariat with weapons for fighting the bourgeoisie." (Emphasis C.M.)

As Marx describes the proletariat becoming politicized and moving toward revolution, he is not describing "winning people to the scientific understanding that *we do not have to live this way.*" He is not describing "putting revolution on the map" so "people throughout society know about this revolution." He is describing material conditions of life becoming more and more unstable and difficult due to the irrational nature of the capitalist system and the advancement of technology ("modern machinery"). He is describing working class people being forced to band together ("begin to form combinations") out of necessity in order to get better pay and treatment from employers. He is describing the ruling class drawing the workers into politics, furnishing them with weapons to overthrow the entire system by becoming politicized.

The revolution Marx envisions comes from a prolonged economic crisis created by the problems of poverty amid plenty, exacerbated by technological advancement. As the conditions get worse, and the working class is left "outcast and starving amid the wonders we have made," the growing "reserve army of labor" will have no choice but to seize the means of production and organize them rationally for the good of society.

The revolution is not created by ideas, just as the deteriorating conditions are not created by a lack of morality on the part of the capitalists. These things flow from the natural working of the system and are resolved by changing property relations. Communists harness the societal energy and waves of resistance to deteriorating economic conditions in order to empower the working class, which is increasingly politicized, to seize control of the centers of economic power. This of course, requires taking hold of state power in order to exercise such authority. While there is certainly a role for individuals and revolutionary organizations in activating the working class amid the crisis and pushing them to fulfill history's challenge, their words and ideas are not the cause of the crisis and upsurge itself, and neither are the bad intentions or immorality of the current order.

Your rhetoric has replaced the economic conditions rooted in the problems of capitalism, the impetus for propelling history forward according to Marx, with a moralistic critique of racism, sexism and political repression. This is a fundamental departure from Marxism.

4. How Can We Achieve The Higher Stage of Communism?

The idealist nature of your worldview is most clearly expressed when you begin articulating your understanding and emphasis on what Marx called "The higher stage of communism." Your work frequently utilizes a formulation from the Cultural Revolution era in China, which describes the ultimate higher stage of communism as "achieving the 4 alls." You summarize it this way: "Marx said specifically the dictatorship of the proletariat is the transition to the abolition of all class distinctions, of all the production relations on which those class distinctions rest, of all the social relations that correspond to those production relations, and the revolutionization of all the ideas that correspond to those social relations."

You go on in the same piece to reflect about what this will look like, as the higher stage of Communism negates money as a means of exchange: "Now, there's still a lot to be understood and in the future to be worked out concretely about how you would do exchange under communism without money. Are you going to have certificates that entitle you to certain things?

Well, then, how do you prevent even those certificates from being turned into capital and the basis to exploit people? You know, in prison you don't have money, but all kinds of things, cigarettes or other things, can become commodities that are used to get an advantage over other people. So a lot of work is going to have to go on to figure out how you do exchange without re-creating the basis for exploitation. But the point is, if you don't get beyond this system of commodity exchanges, and the law of value which regulates them, then you can never implement the slogan of communism, in any full sense. What is that slogan? "From each according to their ability, to each according to their needs." This means that you're not calculating through money any more. Communist society—you won't have it until people have gotten beyond the idea that they need more than somebody else, just to have more than somebody else. And that has to do with the 4th of the "4 Alls," right?—the revolutionization of all the ideas that go along with social relations of oppression and exploitation. But at the base of all this is the system of production relations, the economic system, the mode of production—and you can see how complex this is."

It is apparent that you completely miss the essence of Marx's teaching on this topic. When describing the higher stage of communism and contrasting it with the lower stage, commonly called "socialism," Marx wrote the following in

Critique of the Gotha Program: "But these defects are inevitable in the first phase of communist society as it is when it has just emerged after prolonged birth pangs from capitalist society. **Right can never be higher than the economic structure of society and its cultural development conditioned thereby.** In a higher phase of communist society, after the enslaving subordination of the individual to the division of labor, and therewith also the antithesis between mental and physical labor, has vanished; **after labor has become not only a means of life but life's prime want; after the productive forces have also increased with the all-around development of the individual, and all the springs of co-operative wealth flow more abundantly** – only then can the narrow horizon of bourgeois right be crossed in its entirety and society inscribe on its banners: From each according to his ability, to each according to his needs!" (Emphasis C.M.)

Notice that Marx explains "right can never be higher than the economic structure of society." He

The Communist Party of China has focused on raising living standards as a way of marching toward the higher stage of communism.

says that "From each according to his ability, to each according to his needs" is only possible under specific circumstances. These circumstances are "labor has become not only a means of life but life's prime want," i.e. a society in which technology has advanced to the point in which human beings do not have to work, but only do so voluntarily to entertain themselves, a society in which mental and physical labor are no longer distinguished from each other. He speaks of how the "springs of cooperative wealth flow more abundantly" and "productive forces have also increased with the all-around development of the individual."

All of this is referring to a society with a huge amount of abundance and wealth, so much wealth existing that the need to regulate or ration commodities is completely gone. People can just take whatever they need and do what they feel like doing, from each according to his own abilities, to each according to his needs.

In Marx's historical materialist understanding, each mode of production leads to a higher level of human comfort, a longer life expectancy and an increase in the human population. Slavery, feudalism, and capitalism all significantly raised the level of human productivity and technology when they arose to replace the previous social order, and socialism and eventually communism will do the same. Social relations will be reinvented on the basis of a new level of human comfort and a new level of independence and mastery over nature. The higher stage of communism is the ultimate stage of human productivity and abundance, in which all class dynamics are eliminated.

Vladimir Lenin also explains this in his work *The State and Revolution*: "The economic basis for the complete withering away of the state is such a high state of development of communism at which the antithesis between mental and physical labor disappears, at which there consequently disappears one of the principal sources of modern social inequality--a source, moreover, which cannot on any account be removed immediately by the mere conversion of the means of production into public property, by the mere expropriation of the capitalists. ***This expropriation will make it possible for the productive forces to develop to a tremendous extent. And when we see how incredibly capitalism is already retarding this development, when we see how much progress could be achieved on the basis of the level of technique already attained, we are entitled to say with the fullest confidence that the expropriation*** *of the capitalists will inevitably result in an enormous development of the productive forces of human society.* But how rapidly this development will proceed, how soon it will reach the point of breaking away from the division of labor, of doing away with the antithesis between mental and physical labor, of transforming labor into "life's prime want"--we do not and cannot know." (Emphasis C.M)

Your writing makes the higher stage of communism seem like it is achieved by inculcating society with your communistic principles, by forcing people to live in a new moralistic way. Of course, with such a worldview you are perplexed about how goods can be distributed without recreating some form of currency! But this is not the Marxist-Leninist view at all. The basis for the withering away of the state and all inequality is the absence of any scarcity and the lack of any need to regulate consumption.

5. What Makes A Country Socialist?

You see the higher stage of communism being achieved by "transforming the people" but Marx saw it being achieved on the basis of material conditions. This fundamental misunderstanding you have, where Communism is achieved on a moral plane rather than a material one, fits into your overall idealist world view. By not explaining the problems of capitalism, the way technology leads to economic crisis, poverty amid plenty, and then not explaining socialism as a means of resolving this, you are missing the entire point of Marx's assessment of human conditions and the trajectory of civilization.

Marx observed the built-in problem of production organized for profit as it was emerging from feudalism when he wrote: "In these crises, a great part not only of the existing products, but also of the previously created productive forces, are periodically destroyed. **In these crises, there breaks out an epidemic that, in all earlier epochs, would have seemed an absurdity — the epidemic of overproduction.** Society suddenly finds itself put back into a state of momentary barbarism; it appears as if a famine, a universal war of devastation, had cut off the supply of every means of subsistence; industry and commerce seem to be destroyed; and why? Because there is too much civilization, too much means of subsistence, too much industry, too much commerce. **The productive forces at the disposal of society no longer tend to further the development of the conditions of bourgeois property;** on the contrary, they have become too powerful or these conditions, by which they are fettered, and so soon as they overcome these fetters, they bring disorder into the whole of bourgeois society, endanger the

During the Cultural Revolution, the Gang of Four argued that development was not necessary and China could move toward a "higher stage in poverty."

existence of bourgeois property. The conditions of bourgeois society are too narrow to comprise the wealth created by them. **And how does the bourgeoisie get over these crises? On the one hand by enforced destruction of a mass of productive forces; on the other, by the conquest of new markets, and by the more thorough exploitation of the old ones. That is to say, by paving the way for more extensive and more destructive crises, and by diminishing the means whereby crises are prevented."** (Emphasis C.M.)

Marx saw the socialist revolution as a means of resolving this inherently irrational problem. He describes it this way in the Communist Manifesto: "We have seen above, that the first step in the revolution by the working class is to raise the proletariat to the position of ruling class to win the battle of democracy. **The proletariat will use its political supremacy to wrest, by degree, all**

capital from the bourgeoisie, to centralize all instruments of production in the hands of the State, *i.e.*, of the proletariat organized as the ruling class; and to increase the total productive forces as rapidly as possible." (Emphasis C.M.)

Lenin described it this way: "It is this communist society, which has just emerged into the light of day out of the womb of capitalism and which is in every respect stamped with the birthmarks of the old society, that Marx terms the "first", or lower, phase of communist society. **The means of production are no longer the private property of individuals. The means of production belong to the whole of society.**" (Emphasis C.M.)

Friedrich Engels, articulating Marx's understanding in his pamphlet, *Socialism: Utopian and Scientific* explained socialism, the transitional stage toward the ultimate goal of communism, this way: "The socialized appropriation of the means of production does away, not only with the present artificial restrictions upon production, but also with the positive waste and devastation of productive forces and products that are at the present time the inevitable concomitants of production, and that reach their height in the crises. Further, it sets free for the community at large a mass of means of production and of products, by doing away with the senseless extravagance of the ruling classes of today, and their political representatives. The possibility of securing for every member of society, by means of socialized production, an existence not only fully sufficient materially, and becoming day-by-day more full, but an existence guaranteeing to all the free development and exercise of their physical and mental faculties — this possibility is now, for the first time, here, but *it is here*. **With the seizing of**

the means of production by society, production of commodities is done away with, and, simultaneously, the mastery of the product over the producer. Anarchy in social production is replaced by systematic, definite organization. The struggle for individual existence disappears. Then, for the first time, man, in a certain sense, is finally marked off from the rest of the animal kingdom, and emerges from mere animal conditions of existence into really human ones." (Emphasis C.M.)

For Marx and Engels, the lower stage of communism, commonly called "socialism" was a fundamentally economic question. Capitalism is a system in which the means of production operate in order to make profits for private owners. Socialism is when the means of production are subject to control by society i.e. "Anarchy in social production is replaced by systematic, definite organization" (Engels) "centralize all instruments of production in the hands of the State" (Marx) "The means of production belong to the whole of society" (Lenin).

You see the socialist revolution very differently. For you, it is once again a question of ideas, morality, and a vague sense of democratic participation. In a selection from your work that you have made a point of widely circulating called *Three Alternative Worlds* you contrast your understanding of socialism with what you call "a revisionist society" pointing toward the post-1956 Soviet Union as an example, in which you allege "fundamentally the role of the masses of people is no different than it is under the classical form of capitalism."

For a society to be truly socialist and on the road to Communism, you explain: "it's a society and a world that the great majority of people would actually want to live in. One in which not only do they not have to worry about where their next meal is coming from, or if they get sick whether they're going to be told that they cant have health care because they can't pay for it, as important as that is; but **one in which they are actually taking up, wrangling with, and increasingly making their own province all the different spheres of society.** Achieving that kind of a society, and that kind of a world, is a very profound challenge. It's much more profound than simply changing a few forms of ownership of the economy and making sure that, on that basis, peoples social welfare is taken care of, but you still have people who are taking care of that *for* the masses of people; and all the spheres of science, the arts, philosophy and all the rest are basically the province of a few. And the political decision-making process remains the province of a few. To really leap beyond that is a tremendous and world-historic struggle that we've been embarked on since the Russian revolution (not counting the very short-lived and limited experience of the Paris Commune)--and in which we reached the high point with the Chinese revolution and in particular the Cultural Revolution--but from which we've been thrown back temporarily. So we need to make a further leap on the basis of summing up very deeply all that experience. There are some very real and vexing problems that we have to confront and advance through in order to draw from the best of the past, but go further and do even better in the future."

In presenting this interpretation of the 20th Century, you are upholding the political line of the Chinese government from the final years of the cultural revolution. You argue that the Soviet Union was only a socialist society from 1917 until 1956 when Khruschev the "revisionist" secured his grip on power. Unlike other critics of the Soviet Union, or even Mao until 1970 or so, you do not maintain that the USSR was socialist in its economic foundations but led by corrupt or reformist leaders. You rather maintain that as the result of leaders taking power who have the wrong political understanding and/or operate in a self-serving manner, the USSR reverted to being a capitalist society.

This position which has been repudiated by the Chinese Communist Party and the bulk of Communist Parties in the world that once adhered to it, is idealist nonsense put forward at a time when the leadership of China was fundamentally flawed. There was no dramatic economic shift in the Soviet Union following the 20th Party Congress when Khruschev unleashed his anti-Stalin tirade and shifted toward a foreign policy of seeking detente. The major centers of economic power remained under state control and subject to 5-year-economic plans. There were no mass privatizations and no wave of foreign investment. Nothing changed in the USSR in 1956 other than the leaders began espousing a different understanding of world events, pursuing a different relationship with the western capitalist countries and directing their international allies in the global communist movement to act differently. Arguing that the USSR "restored capitalism" in 1956 is pure idealism. Khruschev did not alter the nature of the soviet economy with his words.

Your goal post for what defines a society to be genuinely socialist ("one in which they are actually taking up, wrangling with, and increasingly making their own province all the different spheres of society") is purely subjective and impossible to really measure. It also has nothing to do with what Marx wrote about or defined socialism to be.

Your vision of a non-revisionist, truly socialist society seems not to be really an economic concept, but rather an aspiration of fulfilling the ideals of bourgeois democracy, "the rule of the people" without any elite or ruling caste dictating policy. Lenin makes clear that pure democracy is only possible with the absence of classes, and abolishing classes means changing the nature of property relations. Your view is reminiscent of the so-called 'Workers Opposition' in the early years of the Russian Revolution, or various ultra-leftist, "council communist" or anarchist critiques of the USSR. You uphold a vision that is more about realizing democratic ideals than altering the mode of production.

6. The Anti-Imperialist World Today

China certainly experienced dramatic economic reforms following the death of Mao

Zedong, starting with the Reform and Opening Up of 1978. However, in China today, the means of production still operate according to a centralized 5-year economic plan. Even the private companies in China are forced to accede to the state's wishes, in the interests of all society, with Communist Party bureaucrats stepping in to direct their actions and no real private property rights existing.

Socialism first came into the world with the 1917 Bolshevik revolution and it rapidly expanded during the Cold War. While there were certainly dramatic setbacks in 1989-1991 when various governments were toppled, socialism still exists in many corners of the globe and has even expanded in the 21st century. Marxist-Leninist parties remain in power and oversee popular control of the means of production in Cuba, Laos, North Korea and Vietnam. I think non-Marxist-Leninist forms of socialism exist as well under the leadership of

Baathist Arab Socialists, Bolivarians, and Islamic Revolutionaries. Pretty much every country that breaks free from the domination of the western financial system, what Lenin called "Imperialism: The highest stage of capitalism" must adopt an economic model where the anarchy of production is replaced by definite systemic organization, and

Communists from around the world gather every four years for the World Festival of Youth and Students.

LETTER TO BOB AVAKIAN

must attach itself to the alternative pole in the global economy centered around China and Russia.

Your analysis of world affairs says that none of these countries measure up to your subjective appraisal that the bulk of the population "are actually taking up, wrangling with, and increasingly making their own province all the different spheres of society," but I would argue even in this criteria they do quite well.

While you defend the Soviet Union before 1956 and China before 1976, your organization's publications routinely take at face value the allegations made against other societies that are at odds with the western imperialists. In doing so, you repeat uncritically the assumption that these societies are brutal authoritarian dictatorships with no democratic participation. As someone who has visited the Islamic Republic of Iran, Nicaragua and

Venezuela among other anti-imperialist states, I must say your assessment of them is fundamentally wrong.

None of the anti-imperialist governments in the world that face constant attempts at regime change and destabilization from the United States would remain in power without the support of a highly organized and politicized population. The basis of Venezuela's revolutionary government is Bolivarian Circles that operate in neighborhoods, much like the Soviets of the USSR. These community-level organizations involve hundreds of thousands of people who are highly involved in decision making and engage in all kinds of debate and discussion as they enforce and carry out the vision for Bolivarian Socialism on a community level. Nicaragua's "Citizen's Power Councils" are similar. The Islamic Republic of Iran depends on local Basij councils for its support, and on a highly politicized and religious military organization called the Islamic Revolutionary Guard Corp, which is the largest economic entity in the country.

The Chinese Communist Party has 90 million members and every corner of this vast, highly populated country has individuals who are closely directed by the Communist Party, consulted by it for information and input, and are themselves essential in enacting its policy goals and formulating its understanding of how to move the country forward.

These governments mobilize their population and involve them in governing out of necessity. Unlike the western capitalist governments and their allies, they cannot count on the de facto complicity of the global media, educational system, and international apparatus in maintaining their system. In order to withstand the barrage of US imperialist subversion and economic warfare; to exist in the face of so much opposition from the western monopolists and their states, these governments must have a very close-knit relationship with their people. They must deliver real improvements in living standards.

They must be responsive to people's concerns and they must have the ability to mobilize the population to achieve their goals and defend their state.

Despite many of these countries certainly not having the same level of civil liberties as is enjoyed by those of us living in the western capitalist countries, these countries, in this sense at least, are more "democratic." When a government that controls an independent economy, facing up against the prevailing western system becomes so reliant on its population's support, it is closer to the ideal of bourgeois democracy "the rule of the people" than a western country where the people are ruled over and managed like a herd of animals. Our rulers in the west and their aligned governments rely on the fact that they are backed up by the tiny, wealthy ultra-rich minority. Governments around the world that have broken free from the western imperialist financial order have no such defacto-preservation or insurance, and they must be more reliant on their people.

Socialism is not synonymous with state ownership, you are correct on this. Socialism is when production no longer functions on the basis of "preliminary transformation into capital" but rather is operated on a planned basis. Governments that have emerged in popular revolutions against the western imperialists on behalf of a well-organized population in which the working class and the peasantry constitute a clear majority, fit the Marxist-Leninist definition of socialism.

Such governments have presided over mobilizing the population to build their countries up with state central planning, industrializing, wiping out illiteracy, electrifying countries and raising societies once chained in poverty by western capitalism to higher and higher levels of development. In doing so, they fulfill the purpose socialism is stated to have by Engels: "securing for every member of society, by means of socialized production, an existence not only fully sufficient materially, and becoming day-by-day more full, but an existence guaranteeing to all the free development and exercise of their physical and mental faculties."

These societies are rescuing themselves from the enforced poverty of imperialism, and raising themselves up closer toward the goal of enough wealth and abundance existing that the higher stage of communism can eventually be achieved.

LETTER TO BOB AVAKIAN

This is an economic transformation based on changes in material realities. It may not measure up to your desire for some kind of spiritual transformation based on what you perceive to be a liberating tone of discourse, mass wrangling with big questions or involvement in decision-making, or the leadership taking the correct political line, but with materialist not idealist analysis, this should not be considered decisive.

There is a logical inconsistency in how you speak about China and the USSR being routinely defamed in US media, yet repeat without a thought or question the defamations of other anti-imperialist states. This inconsistency is particularly disturbing to someone like me who sees opposing imperialism and building solidarity with the forces of global resistance as the duty of all working class people living in western countries.

In some instances, I find this inconsistency particularly glaring. For example, on page 215 of your autobiography *From Ike to Mao and Beyond*, you relate this anecdote from your days working with the Black Panthers: "At that particular time no attack came on the Panther national office in Berkeley, but while we were there some of the Panther members decided to do some political education. This was after Eldridge Cleaver, who had gone into exile, had gone to North Korea and sent back word about how great it was. And I didn't agree with this at all, because I'd done some reading about Kim Il Sung and North Korea, and I viewed Kim Il Sung frankly as more like a feudal monarch than anything having to do with socialism and communism. So when this Panther guy stood up in front of a packed room of people in the Panther national office and started saying, "Well, Eldridge has told us that Kim Il Sung is the real revolutionary—he's much more revolutionary than Mao Tsetung," I just couldn't let that go. Even though I was there to do whatever it took to defend the Panther office if it were attacked, I had to speak up. So I said, "Well, I just don't agree with that, Kim Il Sung is not more revolutionary than Mao. Kim Il Sung is not really revolutionary, and North Korea is not really socialist; Kim Il Sung is not an outstanding communist leader at all, let alone a great leader like Mao."

The way you flat out dismiss a country that was closely aligned with China and the Soviet Union, ruled over by a Marxist-Leninist party, facing thousands of US troops on its border as having "nothing to do with socialism and communism" is misinformed. You feel no need to even offer any evidence to back this up. You just assume that the reader shares the pro-imperialist bias found in US media, so you repeat the standard line.

I also think your memory of this particular incident may be a bit off. You say "I viewed Kim Il Sung frankly as more like a feudal monarch." The primary reason that the DPRK is compared to a feudal monarchy in western propaganda is that after Kim Il Sung's death in 1994, his son Kim Jong Il assumed the position of heads of state, and his grandson Kim Jung-Un now holds this position. People see this as reminiscent of monarchial lineage and hereditary titles.

The reason that Kim Il Sung's descendants have been the heads of state since Kim's death is much more complex. The death of Kim Il Sung in 1994 came at a particularly dark moment. The Soviet Union had just dissolved. North Korea had worked very hard to develop food independence during the 1970s and 80s, which was difficult because the arable land of the peninsula is mainly in the south. The territory above the 38th parallel is very mountainous. Regardless, food self-sufficiency was declared. However, the agricultural system of North Korea depended largely on petroleum, gasoline to run the tractors, power the food processing centers, etc. After the fall of the USSR, the petro-dollar reigned supreme and the DPRK was unable to purchase and import petroleum. This resulted in a horrendous food crisis in which mass deaths of malnutrition took place. North Korea refers to this period as the "arduous march" and it was clear the United States was utilizing food and economic isolation as a weapon with which to foment regime change.

When Kim Il Sung died, the DPRK was facing the most serious attack and societal crisis it had faced since the Korean War itself. People were dying of malnutrition. The imperialists were looking for any weakness or division to exploit. Kim Jong-Il's ascendency to leadership, as the son of the founder of the Korean Workers Party, was a political statement. It was a means of preventing the ruling party from dividing, and signifying that the country remained united around the revolutionary line of its founder. It sent a message to the United States that just as Kim Il Sung had not surrendered, the party's new leadership would not either. This continued with Kim Jong-Un.

The idea that it is a monarchy or somehow a feudal society is an absurd imperialist slur. Feudalism is an economic system in which landowners and serfs produce crops in a society that functions mostly at only an agrarian level of development, not industrialized. North Korea, with its huge steel mills, huge power plants, universal literacy, full electrification, satellites in orbit and massive collective farms with modern tractors is not feudalism by any stretch of the imagination. The population are not serfs, but industrial workers. Land-owning nobles do not extract rent from them. Alleging that an industrialized society with the 20th century Marxist-Leninist political and economic model, that you consider to not be sufficiently socialist and somehow revisionist is therefore "feudalist" is ignorant and lacks analysis from a supposed Marxist. It shows a lack of understanding of what feudalism even is, and how feudalism differs from both socialism, capitalism or "revisionism." It is beneath you. It plays into the propaganda used to justify further economic isolation and threats of regime change.

What I find particularly bizarre is that this anecdote about arguing with Black Panther Party members who admired Kim Il Sung is supposed to have taken place in 1969. This was 25 years before Kim Il Sung died and his son Kim Jong Il assumed leadership of the country. So, on what basis would you have calculated North Korea to be "feudal" at this time? The hereditary succession that is the basis for the claim had not taken place yet.

During these years, North Korea's economy was strong. An article published by BBC news on August 26th, 2008 under the headline "N Korea struggles to control changing economy" confirms this, explaining: "At one time, North Korea's centrally planned economy seemed to work well - indeed, in the initial years after the creation of North Korea following World War II, with spectacular results. The mass mobilization of the population, along with Soviet and Chinese technical assistance and financial aid, resulted in annual economic growth rates estimated to have reached 20%, even 30%, in the years following the devastating 1950-53 Korean war. As late as the 1970s, South Korea languished in the shadow of the "economic miracle" north of the border. In the

West, governments fretted that Communist-backed North Korea was putting the Western-backed, capitalist South to shame."

At the time, Kim Il Sung was only 57 years old. He had been the George Washington of Korea, leading the anti-colonial struggle against Japan and assuming leadership of the post-war government. He had then withstood the horrendous Korean War in which millions of his people were killed, and successfully led post-war reconstruction and rapid industrialization in the following decades. Kim Il Sung was embraced by Mao Zedong who you admired and neutral between the Soviet Union and China in their disagreements. There were strained relations with the Red Guards and Mao's wife Jiang Qing mobilizing protests against him and calling him a "revisionist pig" at one point, but for most of Mao's leadership in China, including most of the period of the Cultural Revolution,

China and North Korea were on friendly terms. Mao Zedong's own son had died in the Korean war, helping to drive US troops back to the 38th parallel.

On what basis would you possibly have dismissed Kim Il Sung as "more like a feudal monarch than anything having to do with socialism and communism" in 1969? Were you clairvoyant, predicting that Kim would die in 1994 and his son would assume the leading position? At the time, US media dismissed North Korea in the same kinds of terms it used for other Marxist-Leninist governments. Accusations of feudalism and the particularly racist and nasty characterizations of the country did not become commonplace in US media until the 1990s, most especially escalating after Bush named them among the "Axis of Evil"in 2002. Did you also have the ability to look into the future and forecast that this would become one of the main central propaganda attacks on the country in the era after the fall of the USSR?

In this mis-recollection of an incident you present yourself as the all-knowing white guy. You present yourself as correcting the mistaken Black Panthers who looked for inspiration to a country that had just welcomed one of their comrades who had fled into exile. To be honest, the whole anecdote and the way present it gives me a rather negative impression of your analysis and leadership style.

You make no mention of North Korea's record of solidarity, not just with the Black Panthers, but also with the Irish Freedom Struggle, Palestinians, the South African Anti-Apartheid movement, and many other anti-imperialist movements, support that is deeply admirable. While you have declared various forces resisting US imperialism around the world to be "revisionist" and "historically out-moded" the Korean Workers Party has a consistent policy of solidarity with all the forces that seek to break free from western domination. I would encourage those who wish to defeat that system to look to them and their allies for inspiration and ideological guidance, rather than to you.

7. Jacobinism not Marxism

I am forced to point out that your definition of socialism, while not consistent with Marxism-Leninism and obscuring materialism and economics, is also fundamentally contradictory. In many places your organization refers to the revolution as being necessary because the leaders of this society and the masses of people have ideas you deem to be reactionary. In *Organizing for Revolution: 7 Key Points* your organization writes: "Brutal and murderous white supremacy, male supremacy, and other oppressive relations, the deepening crisis in society and the world overall, including the constant wars and the continuing destruction of the environment: all this *cannot ultimately be resolved, in any positive way, within the confines of the system that rules in this country and dominates in the world as a whole*—the system of *capitalism-imperialism*. Under the rule of this system, all this will only get worse."

In the hopes of creating a purely egalitarian and democratic society, the Jacobins carried the out the Reign of Terror following the French Revolution.

You contend your revolution is necessary - to get rid of white supremacy, male supremacy, oppressive relations, destruction of the environment - and yet you also argue that a society cannot be socialist unless the people "are actually taking up, wrangling with, and increasingly making their own province all the different spheres of society."

Well, what if the people hold views that are male supremacist? Or white supremacist? What if the people favor the destruction of the environment in order to increase their living standards? In such cases, your revolutionary government, in order to fulfill its stated goal of "uprooting" oppression, would have to disempower the masses of people, and go contrary to your stated criteria for socialism as popular participation in decision-making and widespread "wrangling."

The goal of imposing an egalitarian vision onto society, and the goal of ensuring that masses of people are heavily involved in decision-making and the will of the people is enacted do not always correspond. In fact, they often directly contradict each other. While your organization speaks in the name of "the people," most especially those who are not white as it rallies in support of abortion being kept legal, it forgets that many people of color are vehemently opposed to abortion, seeing it as contrary to Christianity and in some cases, a weapon of white oppressors who seek to exterminate them.

While your organization speaks in the name of "the people" while protesting police brutality, it seems to forget that in addition to the millions of Americans who march with Black Lives Matter, there are also millions who support the cops and rally around the slogan "Blue Lives Matter."

You clearly don't want to embolden these people, empower these people, and enact their will. As you speak in the name of "the people" and condemn various governments around the world as not being genuinely socialist, condemning them as mere welfare states due to a lack of democratic participation, you speak of a need to "transform the people" i.e. mold their worldview and lifestyle to be more in accordance with what you, as the designated leader of the revolution, deem to be more acceptable.

What I see in this blatant contradiction of fetishizing democracy and popular participation while at the same time seeing the people as dangerously backward and in need of being "transformed" is a recipe for mob rule. The French "committee on public safety" that oversaw the brutal atrocities of the reign of terror following the revolution had a similar contradictory view. The

Cultural Revolution in China that you glorify was done in the name of "the people" but often involved the teenage Red Guards terrorizing the population, and behaving in a cruel, punitive manner against those whose words or actions did not conform to what was seen to be in line with Communism.

What is clear is that your revolution's goals seem to have almost completely departed from the economic mission of socializing control of the means of production. You want to fulfill the ideals of bourgeois democracy and enact "the will of the people." You also want to impose your vision of social justice, anti-racism, feminism and egalitarianism onto all of human civilization, "transforming the people" so they will accept it. This is not Marxism by any means. This is not a vision rooted in dialectical and historical materialism. This is the bloodlust of the bourgeois revolutionary intelligentsia. This is William Blake's proclamation that "I shall not cease from mental strife, nor shall my sword sleep in my hand, till we have built Jerusalem."

Your "new Communism" makes this fundamentally clear. You propose that after coming to power you seek to safeguard against "revisionist" leaders betraying revolutionary ideals with similar methods to Mao's cultural revolution or the Jacobin nightmare of the 1790s. You write: "Contradictions within the economic base, in the superstructure, and in the relation between base and superstructure of the socialist countries themselves, as well as the influence, pressure, and outright attacks from the remaining imperialist and reactionary states at any given time, would give rise to class differences and class struggle within a socialist country; these contradictions would constantly pose the possibility of society being led on *either* the socialist *or* the capitalist road, and more specifically would repeatedly regenerate an aspiring bourgeois class, within socialist society itself, which would find its most concentrated expression among those within the Communist Party, and particularly at its highest levels, who adopted *revisionist* lines and policies, which in the name of communism would actually accommodate to imperialism and lead things back to capitalism. Mao identified these revisionists as "people in authority taking the capitalist road," and he pinpointed the struggle between communism and revisionism as the concentrated expression, in the superstructure, of the contradiction and struggle in socialist society between the socialist road and the capitalist road. Mao recognized, and emphasized, that so long as these material conditions and their ideological reflections existed, there could be no guarantee against the reversal of the revolution and the restoration of capitalism, no simple and easy means of preventing this, no solution other than to continue the revolution to restrict and finally, together with the advance of the revolution throughout the world, uproot and eliminate the social inequalities and other vestiges of capitalism that gave rise to this danger... The reversal of socialism and what is in fact the restoration of capitalism in the Soviet Union and China was not a matter of "the revolution eating its own children"...of "conspiratorial communist revolutionists turning into totalitarian tyrants" once they have power...of "bureaucratic leaders, entrenched in power for life, stifling and suffocating (bourgeois) democracy"...it was not "the inevitable result of perpetuating hierarchical organization of society"...or any of the other fundamentally erroneous and unscientific notions which are so ceaselessly propagated these days in attacking communism. Those who directly brought about the defeat of the revolution in the Soviet Union and in China were in fact people with high positions in the revolutionary party and state, but they were not some group of faceless, and classless, bureaucrats, mad for power for its own sake.

They were, as Mao characterized them, people in authority *taking the capitalist road*. They were representatives not of communism but of capitalism, and in particular the vestiges of capitalism that had not yet been thoroughly uprooted and surpassed—and could not be in the short term and within the confines of one or another particular socialist country. The fact that these revisionists were high-ranking officials in the party and state apparatus does not reveal some fundamental flaw in communism or in the communist revolution and socialist society as it has taken shape up to this point. It does not point to the need to find a whole other means and model for bringing about a radically different world. The causes of these reversals of socialism lie deeper, and they are consistent with a scientific communist understanding of society, and in particular of socialism as a transition from capitalism to communism."

In the above passages, what I hear is that this new social order you propose is apparently so fragile, that all it takes for it to be completely unraveled is leadership with the wrong political line holding office. Your idealist worldview that almost completely strips Marxism of its economic understanding and reduces it to a libidinal battle for "liberty, egalite, fraternity" is a recipe for disaster. Furthermore, it seems to have been taken up much more broadly than simply in the ranks of the RCP. Your worldview is in essence a much more ideologically coherent and honest statement of what is believed by most "woke" activists. Society must be more fair and just. People with bad views who oppress others must be punished. "The people" must enact this program with mass mobilizations to hold them accountable.

This vision is certainly playing out across the world, the result being the overthrow of various anti-imperialist states in the Arab Spring and various color revolutions, the increased alienation and confusion among the young people of this country, a brutal call-out and cancel culture that dismantles organizations and overall a move toward liberal atomization and post-modern hopelessness. This very libidinal, anti-authoritarian, mob justice cancel culture has been effectively utilized against your organization in recent years, the very incident that prompted me to write this lengthy critique of your worldview. With little information other than some labels disseminated by mainstream "liberal" capitalist media, social media mobs were mobilized against Sunsara Taylor, simply for being a good anti-Trump activist and mobilizing for abortion.

I am glad to see that these vicious attacks turned into kind of a wake up call for your organization, and that Sunsara Taylor has given great speeches pushing back against woke-ness. You have made comments critiquing wokeness yourself and this is all good. But I think your critique does not go far enough, and this is because your own worldview and the view of the woke mobilized against you have significant overlap.

8. The label of "economism"

The routine justification used by your organization for removing the economics of

Marxism and replacing it with class-less celebration of rebellion and vague calls for uprooting oppression and democratic participation is a denunciation of "economism."

In your autobiography you define economism as "the idea that the key thing is to center everything around the immediate economic struggles of the workers—and toward a "lowest common denominator" kind of politics" on page 203. On page 243 you define it as "a basically trade unionist approach of centering the struggle of the workers around their economic demands and basically reducing the workers' movement to a battle around day-to-day needs." On page 290 you define it as "a view that when you go to the working class, you reduce your politics down to the level of trade-unionism, you make everything revolve just around the day-to-day struggles of the workers for wages and working conditions, and you leave the broader political struggle and beyond that the strategic political and revolutionary goals out of the picture."

The fact that you feel a need to define the concept of "economism" three separate times in the same book shows how central opposing it is to your worldview and the way the Revolutionary Communist Party has developed. You reiterate this on page 385 describing how great it was to break with economism, writing: "To make such a rupture with economism was very revivifying and very liberating for me and for our Party as a whole. Our whole practice changed enormously." You are essentially describing how transitioning your party away from sounding like other communist parties and toward the kind of Jacobinist New Left approach that defines your New Synthesis of today is considered to be one of your greatest achievements.

LETTER TO BOB AVAKIAN

But it must be pointed out that the way you characterize "economism" is fundamentally different from how Vladimir Lenin defined it. Lenin defined the trend of economism as "Economism (in the broad sense of the word), the principal feature of which is its incomprehension, even *defense of lagging*, i.e., as we have explained, the lagging of the conscious leaders behind the spontaneous awakening of the masses. The characteristic features of this trend express themselves in the following: with respect to principles, in a vulgarization of Marxism and in helplessness in the face of modern "criticism", that up-to-date species of opportunism; with respect to politics, in the striving to restrict political agitation and political struggle or to reduce them to petty activities, in the failure to understand that unless Social-Democrats take the leadership of the general democratic movement in *their own* hands, they will never be able to overthrow the autocracy." (A Talk With Defenders of Economism, Dec. 6th, 1901)

Much of Lenin's fundamental tactical book *What Is To Be Done?* centers around opposing Economism. He wrote describing the trend: "in the

The term "Economism" refers to tailing after the labor movement while not raising revolutionary slogans or teaching Marxism.

very first literary expression of Economism we observe the exceedingly curious phenomenon — highly characteristic for an understanding of all the differences prevailing among present day Social Democrats — that the adherents of the "labor movement pure and simple", worshippers of the closest "organic" contacts."

Lenin characterizes economism as "bowing to spontaneity" and "tailism." He describes it as "reducing the role of Social-Democracy to mere subservience to the working-class movement." (Social-Democracy was the label under which Russian Marxists operated at the time.)

Economism is not simply raising economic demands, analyzing the economy, or agitating around economic conditions. Economism is characterized by not calling for the overthrow of capitalism, not spreading an overall Marxist worldview, but merely focusing on day to day labor activism. Economism more or less means not offering leadership in the ideological or tactical sense, and following behind forces in the labor movement. Lenin wrote: "What was the source of our disagreement? It was the fact that on questions both of organization and of politics the Economists are forever lapsing from Social-Democracy into trade-unionism. The political struggle of Social-Democracy is far more extensive and complex than the economic struggle of the workers against the employers and the government." He goes on to contrast the role of a trade union with the kind of revolutionary "party of new type" he advocates: "The workers' organization must in the first place be a trade union organization; secondly, it must be as broad as possible; and thirdly, it must be as public as conditions will allow… On the other hand, the organization of the revolutionaries must consist first and foremost of people who make revolutionary activity their profession…In view of this common characteristic of the members of such an organization, *all distinctions as between workers and intellectuals*, not to speak of distinctions of trade and profession, in both categories, *must be effaced.*"

To use the Leninist critique of reformism, tailism and failure to provide leadership is completely dishonest. Lenin did not call for chucking Marx's critique of the capitalist economy and its problems of overproduction and the tendency of the rate of profits to fall. Lenin did not call for the material basis of the higher stage of communism to be completely forgotten. Lenin did not advocate redefining socialism to be some kind of fulfillment of bourgeois democratic ideals about popular political participation combined with the imposition of an egalitarian social vision.

"Economism" simply does not refer to all discussion of or understanding of Marxist economics. Opposing "economism," at least for Lenin, did not include stripping Marxism of its economic content, which is fundamental.

Karl Marx began his writing as a philosopher, drawing from the Hegelian trend to criticize religion and authoritarianism. By 1848 Marx was a political activist, composing the Communist Manifesto and organizing the Communist League to participate in the German Revolution with a mission of mobilizing the proletariat to fight for its liberation. Marx spent the bulk of his career as a writer often doing his research in the British Museum in London, compiling economic data and statistics and assembling the content of the four volumes of Capital (*Das Kapital*), most of which would be published posthumously.

Your organization proclaims your "New Synthesis" to be of a higher caliber than Marx, Lenin or even Mao, a "new stage" in the communist revolution. For these claims to be made while you demonstrate a consistent lack of knowledge of the basic economic content of Marxism, so much so that you do not even properly define feudalism and dismiss understanding or discussion of the laws of capitalist production as "economism" makes this very hard to accept.

9. Imperialism is a system

One of the areas where your lack of interest in economics or economic analysis is the most glaring and leads you the furthest off the mark is the issue of imperialism. In common language, imperialism roughly means "one country attacking or controlling another country" or "when you construct an empire." However, for adherents of Marxism-Leninism it has a specific definition as referring to an economic system.

For Marxist-Leninists, imperialism is not a verb, it is a noun. It is not something you do, it is not a policy or an action a government takes. Imperialism is a global economic system. Your organization seems to understand this on some level, frequently referring to the U.S. system as "capitalism-imperialism" in various publications.

Lenin offered this definition when laying out his new concept of imperialism as capitalism in its monopolistic stage. He wrote: "We have to begin with as precise and full a definition of imperialism as possible. Imperialism is a specific historical stage of capitalism. Its specific character is threefold: imperialism is monopoly capitalism; parasitic, or decaying capitalism; moribund capitalism. The supplanting of free competition by monopoly is the

LETTER TO BOB AVAKIAN

fundamental economic feature, the *quintessence* of imperialism. Monopoly manifests itself in five principal forms: **(1) cartels, syndicates and trusts**—the concentration of production has reached a degree which gives rise to these monopolistic associations of capitalists; **(2) the monopolistic position of the big banks**—three, four or five giant banks manipulate the whole economic life of America, France, Germany; **(3) seizure of the sources of *raw material* by the trusts and the financial oligarchy** (finance capital is monopoly industrial capital merged with bank capital); **(4) the (economic) partition of the world by the international cartels** has *begun*. There are already over *one hundred* such international cartels, which command the *entire* world market and divide it "amicably" among themselves—until war *re*divides it. The export of capital, as distinct from the export of commodities under nonmonopoly capitalism, is a highly characteristic phenomenon and is closely linked with the economic and territorial-political partition of the world; **(5) the territorial partition of the world** (colonies) is *completed*." (Emphasis C.M.)

Lenin presents an understanding of a system of "cartels, syndicates and trusts," a "financial oligarchy," that carry out the "partition of the world." He lays out that the "export of capital" rather than the "export of commodities" is highly

Communists seek to build solidarity with the people of the world and defeat imperialism.

linked with this seizing of territory across the planet. In essence, according to Lenin, imperialism means big banks and huge corporations holding back economic development and seizing chunks of the world as captive markets.

As Lenin explains in his piece *Imperialism and the Split in Socialism*, the struggle against imperialism defines the revolutionary movement in our time. Lenin wrote with passion about how pro-imperialist "socialists" and labor leaders, based among sections of the working class that had effectively been bought off with higher wages ("the aristocracy of labor") were the principal enemy of the working class movement, explaining: "The bourgeoisie of an imperialist "Great" Power *can economically* bribe the upper strata of "its" workers by spending on this a hundred million or so francs a year, for its *super*profits most likely amount to about a thousand million." Lenin explained that the First World War was enabled to happen because a layer of pro-imperialist sellout socialist leaders had directed the working class not to oppose it, but rally around their imperialist bosses. This led to 20 million workers being sent to their deaths.

He explained that mobilizing in opposition to pro-imperialist elements in the working class movement was essential : "The point is that at the present time, in the imperialist countries of Europe, *you are fawning* on the opportunists, who are *alien* to the proletariat as a class, who are the servants, the agents of the bourgeoisie and the vehicles of its influence, and *unless* the labor movement *rids* itself of them, it will remain a *bourgeois labor movement*. By advocating "unity" with the opportunists, with the Legiens and Davids, the Plekhanovs, the Chkhenkelis and Potresovs, you are, objectively, defending the

LETTER TO BOB AVAKIAN

enslavement of the workers by the imperialist bourgeoisie with the aid of its best agents in the labor movement. The victory of revolutionary Social-Democracy on a world scale is absolutely inevitable, only it is moving and will move, is proceeding and will proceed, *against* you, it will be a victory *over* you."

Lenin argued that instead of trying to court and win over the pro-imperialist "socialists" it was correct for communists to look past them, and win over the sections among the working people who are suffering and not bought off by imperialist crumbs. He wrote: "it is therefore our duty, if we wish to remain socialist to **go down *lower and deeper*, to the real masses**; this is the whole meaning and the whole purport of the struggle against opportunism." (Emphasis C.M.)

All of this is vitally important in our time, because the primary error of not just you but the bulk of the global communist movement is aligning with the imperialist bourgeoisie in their crusade against Russia and China, and doing so on the basis that they are "imperialists." Every Marxist-Leninist government in the world supports Russia and China against the imperialists. The Korean Workers Party, Communist Party of Vietnam, the Lao People's Revolutionary Party, the United Socialist Party of Venezuela, the Sandinistas National Liberation Front, the Communist Party of Cuba, etc. Not a single ruling Communist Party has been neutral or taken a pro-NATO stance in the current conflict in Ukraine. British Communist leader Joti Brar has heroically formed the World Anti-Imperialist Platform, a regroupment of international communist forces pushed by the Korean People's Democracy Party, as a way to rally communists toward an anti-imperialist position, in alliance with the existing communist states.

The reason the World Anti-Imperialist platform is so important is because among the various Communist and Marxist organizations of the west there has been a complete betrayal of anti-imperialist principles. The Communist Party of Greece (KKE), a longtime stalwart of anti-revisionism, has lurched into neutrality. The Anarchists, Maoists and Trotskyites and various "revolutionary" trends in the west have all more or less lined up with the US state department or become neutral. This is no doubt due to two major factors. First, the infiltration and manipulation of these groups by intelligence services, a process that began during the Cold War and is now public record. Second, the hysterical reaction of the middle class in the western world that quivers in fear of the populist "New Right."

I believe your organization has taken its stance for both of these reasons and the remainder of this letter will provide evidence as to why.

I must say, the Revolutionary Communist Party's position is far better than that of the Communist Party USA, the Democratic Socialists of America and most other so-called leftist organizations in America. Most so-called "socialist" voices in America, taking their cues from the AFL-CIO leadership, Alexandria Ocasio-Cortez and Bernie Sanders are cheering for more weapons to be sent to Ukraine, more provocations on Taiwan, and a further escalation against the anti-imperialist countries. They do so on the basis that Putin is "right-wing" for allegedly supporting Trump, that China is "racist" in supposedly oppressing Uyghurs. In the name of "social justice" we are told that the human rights focused, enlightened western imperialist powers must be supported against the "backward" Russians and Chinese.

This is nothing more than a repackaging, of course, of Neocon George W. Bush's claim that he invaded Iraq to 'give the Iraqi people a chance at freedom.' It is the "white man's burden" logic of colonizers and oppressors from the beginning of time, much as slave-masters claimed they were being charitable by dragging Black people from Africa, as they were "civilizing them" and "teaching them Christianity."

Fighting for an anti-imperialist position today is just as vitally important as it was in 1914. Humanity is on the brink of a new world war, and if such a war breaks out Russia and China must win and the western imperialist powers must lose. Any other outcome would be completely devastating for the future of the human race. Clarity on this point must be established.

10. Russia and China are NOT imperialists

Your organization has heroically called out the hypocrisy of those liberal voices who have become jingoistic and anti-Russian. You have warned about the danger of a new world war. You have highlighted the concept of revolutionary defeatism, pointing out that Marxism-Leninism teaches that we must never rally behind our own imperialist bourgeoisie. Yet, at the same time you push against the outright pro-imperialist moves of much of the left, you still maintain neutrality. You claim that Russia and China are themselves "imperialists." However, your own words clearly indicate why Russia does not fit Lenin's definition of imperialism.

In a selection from an interview with you, posted to "The Revcoms" youtube channel on February 22, 2023 entitled "Bob Avakian on Biden,

Putin & Xi Jinping: Imperialist Gangsters and the Need for Revolution!" You gave the following explanation for Russia's recent military operation. You said: "Russia went through the whole thing where the Soviet Union imploded it hadn't been socialist for a long time but it had been pretending to be socialist and then eventually gave that up and the Soviet Union went out of existence and Russia became very weak they had that guy Yeltsin in there who could hardly stay sober for a day as a head of state and Russia became basically just a very subordinate to the U.S and to the whole quote-unquote Western Alliance and ever since Putin came in his whole program has been to reassert you know Russian first of all Russian Integrity but also just Russian influence in the world you know as an imperialist power which is what it is it's a it's a openly capitalist and imperialist power and it's trying to break out of the the subordinate position that it's been in since particularly since the disintegration of the Soviet Union and so this explains what he's been doing he went into Georgia and a number of years back and now into into Ukraine."

Yes, after the fall of the Soviet Union, Russia was subjected to international looting and economic devastation. 30% unemployment, millions living in extreme poverty, a mass rise in drug addiction and human trafficking. The population of Russia actually decreased by roughly 10% during those years.

Vladimir Putin ascended to power in 1999 and began to restructure Russia's economy around state-controlled oil and gas. Russia exports its oil and gas and uses the revenue to subsidize a domestic economy. Russia has state run mining corporations, government subsidized airlines, and a big private sector as well. The Communist Party exists as the largest opposition party to Putin's United Russia Party. The Russian Orthodox Church is the state religion. Pride in the defeat of the Nazis and the accomplishments of the Soviet period accompanies a nationalistic narrative of the great Czars and thousands of years of civilization among the slavic peoples.

Russia is certainly not "socialist" in the sense it was at the time the Soviet Union existed. But to call Russia "imperialist" is misleading. An economy in which the primary source of revenue is the proceeds of domestic natural resources exported to other countries is completely opposite of Lenin's concept of the "export of capital." Russia is not holding back economic development, partitioning corners of the world for itself. Russia's primary trading partners, especially since the escalation in the Donbass region, are Marxist and anti-imperialist governments. Russia's relationship with African countries and countries that have joined the Eurasian Economic Union is simply not one of holding back development. Russia does not have a colonial relationship with these countries, but the opposite. It is spending large amounts of its resources to stabilize and build up these countries, and it is trading with them and offering them military assistance out of mutual necessity.

Russia's state run industries in oil, gas and mining are not pushing the domestic corporations of the countries Russia aligns with out of business, but doing the opposite. Russia has enabled Syria's state run natural gas sector to expand. Russia has helped African countries to expand their domestic mining corporations and better profit from their own resources. If Russia was imperialist, it would be "exporting capital" and Gazprom, Rosneft etc. would be pushing smaller countries out of the market and forcing them to import Russian oil and gas. Russia's economic relationship is simply not one of territorial partition driven by the monopolistic position of big banks.

Russia is a country that has been plundered by the imperialists, but ripped itself free from their domination to rebuild itself economically. Russia stopped being a captive market, a playground for Wall Street and London, and became a competitor on the oil and gas markets. As a result it is under attack.

You dismiss Russia as an imperialist without thorough analysis of its economy, almost as if you are nervously trying to reassure liberals you are not a Putin supporter. Much like your callous dismissal of Kim Il Sung as a "feudal monarchy" you pander to people's anti-communist and pro-imperialist bias. Your rhetoric relies so much on appeasing liberal sensibilities. Phrases like "I wouldn't want to live in those countries" or "That's not the kind of society I would want to live in" can be found all across your writing.

These vague feelings about whether or not a society is "liberating" or not do not measure the objective reality of whether an economy functions in an imperialist manner or not. Russia is not an imperialist country, and neither is China.

China has constructed high speed railway across the planet.

China's economy is largely state run with 5-year-plans and vast state run banks and industries. Inequality certainly exists and corruption has been a problem as well. But China is not making super profits at the expense of the countries it trades with. The Belt and Road initiative, funded by the Asian Infrastructure Investment Bank is an example of win-win cooperation. An example here or there of a Chinese corporation demanding special treatment in exchange for a loan, or mistreatment of employees at the hands of a Chinese corporation does not change the overall nature of Chinese trade. Chinese corporations are not "partitioning the world." China is not ruled by trusts, cartels and syndicates.

China is not ruled by a financial oligarchy, but by the Communist Party which has 90-million members. The Communist Party frequently imprisons and otherwise suppresses millionaires and billionaires within the private sector. To whatever degree China has a "financial oligarchy" it lives in terror of the Communist Party, which frequently suppresses it and forces the economy to function contrary to the laws of the market, in alignment with the overall state central plan.

The focus of the Chinese Communist Party has been poverty alleviation, both in China and around the world. The Chinese Communist Party has repudiated the notion held by the Gang of Four, that China could reach "a higher stage in poverty," but reasserted what Marx made clear in *Critique of the Gotha Program*. The basis for breaking down inequality and the state is raising productive forces. You cannot create communism by willing it or having the correct political line. Communism is to be achieved by unleashing the productive forces from the restraints of capitalism, and allowing them to soar toward abundance.

LETTER TO BOB AVAKIAN

The imperialists are focused on keeping the world poor, so they can stay rich. They are obsessed with "degrowth," bemoaning overpopulation and using climate alarmism as the excuse to stop power plants from being constructed and hold back development. Imperialism has always been about holding back development, but amid the capitalist crisis it has escalated into a frenzy of fascistic economic policies. The imperialists want to drive down the human population, reduce consumption, reduce crop outputs, and rescue capitalism from the prolonged crisis of overproduction. China and Russia want the opposite, they seek development with the oversight of state central planners. This contradiction, between the imperialists and the anti-imperialist block is the main contradiction in the world today.

11. Opposing Imperialism is our duty

In 1961, the Communist Party of China published and circulated a document called *Long Live Leninism!* The text was intended as a subtle critique of the Soviet Union. In the document they articulated Lenin's teachings and they summarized the duty of revolutionaries living in the imperialist centers, people like us: "The liberation movements of the proletariat in the capitalist countries should ally themselves with the national liberation movements in the colonies and dependent countries; this alliance can smash the alliance of the imperialists with the feudal and comprador reactionary forces in the colonies all dependent countries, and will therefore inevitably put a final end to the imperialist system throughout the world."

Defeating the imperialists is the primary duty of communists living in the western countries. It is our task to align the liberation movement of the working class in our countries with the national liberation movements around the world. It is our job to get working people in the United States to see that Russia and China are their allies against the billionaire financial oligarchy that mobilizes them for war and is driving down their living standards. We must build an anti-imperialist layer of US society.

This understanding goes back further than Lenin. Karl Marx explained in 1870 that the working class of Britain must align with the Irish freedom struggle. He wrote in his "Letter to Sigfrid Meyer and August Vogt" in April of 1870: "All industrial and commercial centers in England now have a working class *divided* into two *hostile* camps, English proletarians and Irish proletarians.

The ordinary English worker hates the Irish worker as a competitor who forces down the standard of life. In relation to the Irish worker, he feels himself to be a member of the *ruling nation* and, therefore, makes himself a tool of his aristocrats and capitalists *against Ireland*, thus strengthening their domination *over himself*....England, as the metropolis of capital, as the power that has hitherto ruled the world market, is for the present the most important country for the workers' revolution and, in addition, the *only* country where the material conditions for this revolution have developed to a certain state of maturity. Thus, to hasten the social revolution in England is the most important objective of the International Working Men's Association. The sole means of doing so is to make Ireland independent. **It is, therefore, the task of the "International" to bring the conflict between England and Ireland to the forefront everywhere,**

LETTER TO BOB AVAKIAN

and to side with Ireland publicly everywhere. The special task of the Central Council in London is to **awaken the consciousness of the English working**

Communists seek to align the working class of the imperialist homelands with the colonized peoples of the world fighting for national liberation.

class that, *for them, the national emancipation of Ireland* is not a question of abstract justice or humanitarian sentiment, but *the first condition of their own social emancipation.*" (Emphasis C.M.)

The working people of America who are losing their jobs and homes, must see that the same big banks and corporations trying to push Russia and China off the global market are also looting their communities. The same corporations that profit from piling weapons into Kiev and Tel Aviv are militarizing the police departments of America and feeding the mass incarceration system. The same media that spreads propaganda to justify wars against Russia and China is poisoning the minds of our youth with pessimism, hopelessness, and a shallow culture that values money above all else. The defeat of NATO's puppet foot soldiers in Kiev will be a victory for the working people of America, a defeat for their oppressors and exploiters. Just as Marx said the English communists should mobilize workers to support Ireland against their bosses in the factories, we must mobilize American workers to support Russia and China against the financial oligarchy that rules our country and is driving it into deeper poverty. It is our duty to constantly make clear that the interests of the bulk of America's people do not align with the interests of the imperialist financial oligarchy, but rather with the rising anti-imperialist camp.

After the Second World War the Communist Party of the United States understood its mission to be the construction of an anti-monopoly coalition against the imperialists. The farmers, the Black community, the labor movement, the small business owners, the defenders of democratic rights against fascism, those opposed to war-mongering were to be unified in a solid block of resistance led by the Communist Party. The goal would be the election of a progressive, anti-imperialist government in Washington DC. The concept of the "Anti-Monopoly Coalition" was first put forward by William Z. Foster.

If such an "Anti-Monopoly Government" came to power, Foster explained: "our party contends that such an anti-fascist, anti-war, democratic coalition government, once in power, would be compelled either to move to the Left or to die. **With state power in its hands, it would be forced to pass over from the more or less defensive program upon which it was elected to an offensive policy.** Confronted with the sabotage and open resistance of big business, it would have no other alternative than this, if it hoped to realize any of the progressive legislation of its program and to ensure its staying in power. A people's government would be forced to proceed directly to curb and undermine the power of the monopolies by adopting far-reaching policies of nationalization of the banks and major industries, the break-up of big landholdings, the beginnings of a planned economy, the elimination of reactionary elements from the control of the army, schools, and industry, as well as various other measures to weaken monopoly and to strengthen the working class as the leading progressive force in the nation... **a democratic, anti-fascist, anti-war government, under the violent attacks of the capitalists and in its efforts to find solutions to the burning economic and political problems, if it were to survive, would necessarily move leftward, towards socialism**, much as the People's Democracies of Eastern and Central Europe are now doing." (Emphasis C.M.)

12. Divisions in the ruling class, strategic alliances

In a very recent article you made clear that you understand very well that revolutions involve this kind of polarization and coalition building. You are not like Trotskyites or other ultra-leftists that ramble about "working class independence" and turn their noses up at the notion of a United Front. You understand that United Fronts are an essential aspect of the socialist revolutions that have taken place.

In an article published July 10th, 2023 entitled "Revolution: Major Turning Points and Rare Opportunities" you used the example of the First World War in Russia and Japan's invasion of China as pivotal moments that opened the door for Communists to take power. Explaining the history of China's revolution: "as a result of the invasion

LETTER TO BOB AVAKIAN 143

and occupation of large parts of China by Japanese imperialism, it became both necessary and possible to rally broad sections of the Chinese people in opposition to this invasion and occupation. And the need for the broadest possible resistance against the Japanese occupation, as well as the weakened position of Chiang Kai-shek's government as a result of this occupation, established both the necessity and the basis to enter into a united front with this Chiang Kai-shek government to fight the Japanese invaders... **In a real sense, the Japanese invasion and occupation of China constituted a kind of "fulcrum," shifting the terms of the revolutionary struggle and providing the objective basis for a crucial advance of the revolution, after the devastating setback**...This is what Mao meant when he said that Japan should be thanked for invading China. Obviously, Mao was not unaware of, or unconcerned about, the terrible atrocities which Japan's occupation forces imposed on the Chinese people. His point was that the Japanese invasion and occupation, with all the destruction and suffering it brought for hundreds of millions of Chinese people, and for the Chinese nation as a whole, ended up contributing, in a major way, to the eventual victory of the Chinese revolution, and with it the possibility of uprooting the fundamental and overall causes of the horrific exploitation and oppression to which the masses of Chinese people had been subjected not just for years and decades but for centuries and millennia. *Mao's ironic statement—we should thank Japan for invading—reflects the reality that the invasion and occupation of China by Japanese imperialism ended up contributing, in a major way, to the success of the Chinese revolution.* **But this revolution could not have succeeded if those leading it, and in**

particular Mao, had not grasped and acted in accordance with the changing objective conditions brought about by the Japanese invasion and occupation, particularly as this took place in the overall context of World War 2—and then the qualitatively changed conditions again, within China and in the world as a whole, with the end of World War 2, in which Japan was defeated and its occupation of China ended." (Emphasis C.M.)

You are absolutely correct. The Chinese Flag today represents the "Block of Four Great Classes" that Mao created. The big star represents the Communist Party, and four smaller stars represent the peasants, the workers, the small farmers and the national capitalists. The Communist Party led a block of four great classes with its proletarian ideology. The Communists polarized Chinese society against the Japanese invaders and eventually against all the imperialists, and positioned themselves as the leaders of the New Democratic Revolution, breaking the whole country free from foreign domination.

From there, your article goes on to correctly point out that US society is becoming heavily polarized. You observe, mostly correctly: "the deepening crisis in society and the world overall, including the constant wars and the continuing destruction of the environment: all this *cannot ultimately be resolved, in any positive way, within the confines of the system that rules in this country and dominates in the world as a whole*—the system of *capitalism-imperialism*. Under the rule of this system, all this will only get worse. The deepening divisions within this country now, from top to bottom, mean that those who have ruled in this country for so long (the capitalist-imperialist ruling class) can no longer rule, as a "unified force," in the "normal" way that people have been conditioned to accept—with a system of government that has an outer shell of "democracy" to cover over the fact that it is an actual capitalist *dictatorship* at its core, relying fundamentally on the armed force of the institutions of "official violence," the police and the military. "

You fail to grasp that the crisis is a result of technology and the problem of overproduction

The RCP has built the "Refuse Fascism" organization to support Biden and the Democrats against Donald Trump.

rooted in capitalist production, and seem to accept the climate alarmism promoted by the ultra-rich. However, your assessment of the overall situation is correct. The ruling class is fighting among itself and moving to collapse the open, liberal democratic nature of US society into illiberal authoritarianism in response to a long-term crisis.

However, after that, your article goes awry. You declare: "Because of big changes in this country and the world overall, one part of the ruling class, represented by the Republican Party, has become *fascist*: they no longer believe in or feel bound by what have been the "norms" of "democratic" capitalist rule in this country. And the other section of the ruling class, represented by the Democratic Party, has no real answer to this—except trying to maintain the "normal way" that the oppressive rule of this system has been enforced for hundreds of years, while the fascists are determined to tear up those "norms."

You have this almost exactly wrong. Which party has just indicted the leaders of the African People's Socialist Party, calling them "Russian Agents" and threatening them with 10 years in prison for simply protesting the flow of weapons to Kiev? Biden's justice department is in the process of doing what Trump would never have dreamed of doing, and sending Black revolutionary activists to prison, not for any crime other than anti-war activism, which has earned them the label of "Russian Agents" "interfering" in American politics.

What party has been censoring and manipulating social media in order to change public opinion in its favor? What party wants to make it mandatory for children to be put on hormone blockers and life-altering medications, even if their parents object? What party is leading the charge for escalating hostility to Russia and China?

Donald Trump, who would most likely win and become President again if the vote were taken today, is facing a federal indictment in order to keep him off the ballot. Hundreds of Trump's supporters are in federal prison, after the FBI entrapped them into going into the US capitol building.

The FBI actively went to the owners of Facebook and Twitter and told them to suppress a true story about Hunter Biden's corrupt international dealings as revealed on his laptop, in order to make sure Biden was re-elected in 2020. The Twitter Files, recently released by Elon Musk to journalist Matt Taibbi have revealed that the tech monopolies are working hand in hand with the Democratic Party to suppress voices of opposition and control discourse. The FBI was directly involved in the process.

The threat of establishing an authoritarian state, outlawing dissent and moving the US toward being an illiberal, militarized society is largely coming from the Democrats, not the Republicans.

Fascism is certainly a factor as well, but your understanding of fascism, much like your understanding of socialism and communism, has been stripped of economics. Donald Trump can only be called a "fascist" if you believe fascism is a set of ideas or beliefs. Trump is a bigot. Trump is a racist. Trump is a conservative. Trump may have been quite ugly in his rhetoric. However, Trump's administration more or less represented the lower levels of capital resisting the clampdown from the ultra-rich, not much more.

Fascism, as explained brilliantly by British Communist leader R. Palm Dutt, is the collapse of liberal democracy into authoritarianism amid an economic crisis. Fascism utilizes state power and mass mobilizations of the population to enforce degrowth economic policies in order to reboot the economy. Dutt explained that fascist governments invent the ideology as they go along, in order to justify their policies. He wrote: "Fascism, in fact, developed as a movement in practice, in the conditions of threatening proletarian revolution, as a counter-revolutionary mass movement supported by the bourgeoisie, employing weapons of mixed social demagogy and terrorism to defeat the revolution and build up a strengthened capitalist state dictatorship; and only later endeavored to adorn and rationalize this process with a "theory." **It is in this actual historical process that the reality of Fascism must be found, and not in the secondary derivative attempts post-festum at adornment with a theory.** No less unsatisfactory are the attempted anti-Fascist interpretations of Fascism in terms of ideology or abstract political conceptions." (Emphasis C.M.)

Fascism is the creation of an authoritarian state to reboot the capitalist economy. The American white supremacist Lothrap Stoddard, who visited Nazi Germany, explained the methods the Nazis used to jumpstart their economy: "How did the Nazis actually finance their ambitious projects without currency nor price inflation? They did it in a number of ways. Fluid capital was regimented and either invested according to orders or diverted into government loans. Profits were skimmed off by basic taxation. Above all, consumption was kept down and living standards were lowered by what was called a process of reverse inflation... The upshot has been that the German people have financed astounding expenditures by literally taking it out of their own hides."

With the backing of Hjalamar Schacht, the Krupps and Thyssens, Adolf Hitler seized power and created a slave labor underclass. He restarted military spending. He shamed women out of the workforce. He canceled debt payments to American and British banks and for war reparations under the Versailles treaty. He built a network of highways across the country. All of this eradicated unemployment and temporarily resolved the crisis of overproduction, getting the economy going again and winning the loyalty of the population. The Nazis promoted manual labor and rejected technological innovation. The Nazis utilized slave labor to reboot the German economy, and after the war started they began forcibly depopulating the regions they conquered. The horrendous crimes of the holocaust involved taking every last bit of clothing and property from those gassed to death. The essence of Nazi

LETTER TO BOB AVAKIAN

economics and fascism itself is degrowth. Fascism is "capitalism in decay." It is the capitalist system becoming desperately cannibalistic and regressive, trying to force back the productive forces, in an attempt to resolve the inherent problems created by technological advancement and the irrational profit-centered system.

These economic policies have nothing in common with what Trump did as President. Trump's economic policies mimicked those of Bush. He cut taxes on the rich. He allowed drilling on federal lands. He increased the military budget. However, the economic program of Biden and his closest allies fits the scientific and economic definition of fascism pretty well. The corporation known as BlackRock is actively requiring countries to decrease their crop output in order to receive financing. The 'Green New Deal' seeks to reduce energy consumption dramatically across the

United States. Talk of "overpopulation," a long favored term of white supremacists and eugenicists is widespread. Biden's administration is littered with individuals such as Tracy Stone-Manning who openly speak of depopulation as a necessity. Biden has been escalating military support for the Nazi sympathizers in Kiev, and increases hostility to China.

Donald Trump said a lot of racist things. Donald Trump certainly appeals to the authoritarian and right-wing tendencies of many Americans. But Donald Trump's presidency was overwhelmingly defensive, rolling back Obama-era economic regulations and trying to hold back, to a limited degree, the demand for all out war against Russia and China, the suppression of civil liberties, and push for economic degrowth policies.

Joe Biden's closest allies and advisors all see fascistic economic policies, reducing consumption as an urgent necessity and want as big of a confrontation with Russia and China as possible. They want to silence those who oppose it with social media censorship and in some cases, imprisonment. The Uhuru case is the most serious example. It is a test case to see if prosecutions of people like you and me, people who would oppose the war drive, can move ahead.

There is a big division in the ruling class, but Biden is the fascist. Trump and his supporters represent the lower levels of capital, resisting it with their often racist, bigoted and economically libertarian worldview. Among them, the defensive MAGA wing of the ruling class, there is far more support for Julian Assange, far more support for peace with Russia, than among Biden supporters. Tucker Carlson, before being taken off the air, even defended the Uhuru 3 and called for the charges against them to be dropped.

Though most of the established right-wing are hopeless, typical defenders of the US power structure, among the lower levels of capital and those within the state who have found themselves at odds with the degrowth "globalist" i.e. imperialist agenda, there is more opposition to war and defense of civil liberties than anywhere else. The conservative wing of the political spectrum now has far more diversity, far more opposition to war, far more defense of civil liberties, and far more sympathy with the forces resisting imperialism around the world than the so-called "left."

Your organization is not wrong to see divisions in the ruling class as an opening for potential revolution. The Revolutionary Communist Party has effectively rendered itself to be a politically relevant force due to maneuvering within the divisions in the ruling class. The "Refuse Fascism" organization has had ads in *The New York Times*, and has had nationally televised interviews. Dr. Cornel West has appeared with you at public events, and featured you on his nationally syndicated radio program. The relative success the RCP has had over the years, in relation to other communist organizations, has been due, in part, to its strategic efforts to align with one faction of the ruling class against the other.

I am sure it is knowledge of these intensifying divisions that pushed you to formally endorse Joe Biden in the 2020 election. I was shocked to see this, as your organization has historically forbidden its members from voting and abstained from electoral activism. However, you will notice, this endorsement of Biden and alliance with the dominant liberal faction against Trump's rebellion from the lower levels of capital, did not protect you in the summer of 2022. In the aftermath of the US Supreme Court ruling on abortion, the RCP swung into action and instead of being defended or even accepted by the liberals, you got canceled. Sunsara Taylor's name was dragged through the mud, along with you. Pro-Choice groups signed statements denouncing you. Hit pieces were run in numerous mainstream publications.

Why did they respond to your dedicated, partisan activism in this way? They were sending you a pretty clear message. Biden was making clear 'We don't want your help.' I would assume this is because your organization has somewhat limited, but definitely solid anti-imperialist politics. I would also assume that is because you are an asset, not of the American intelligence community, as most leftist groups are, but other forces. I will discuss this later.

What you don't seem to understand is that the Democratic Party has now assumed the role the Republicans played during the late Cold War. The

LGBT obsessed, climate alarmist, regime change, human rights propaganda-focused "woke" apparatus of NGOs and professional "activists," which has always been funded by the higher levels of capital such as the Rockefellers, the Carnegies and the Duponts; the forces who backed Carter against Reagan in 1980; these forces have become the primary ideological battering ram utilized by the imperialists in our time. They push wars in the name of regime change, they push degrowth in the name of climate change, they push censorship in the name of opposing bigotry and protecting marginalized groups and also in the name of some vague "anti-fascism." The forces that are moving to protect the US imperialist establishment see you as their enemy, not as a useful ally against Trump.

I find it somewhat humorous that your pamphlet on *The Coming Civil War*, written during the Bush years, was the center of right-wing conspiracy theories about "antifa super soldiers." The pamphlet was out of date, but pointed to the illiberalism of the Bush administration and the direction it was moving things in 2005 amid divisions in the ruling class.

I think your pamphlet was mostly correct in those years, and the premise that divisions in the ruling class could lead to a catastrophic event like a civil war in the United States is correct. But let me ask you, if indeed a civil war did break out in the next few years between the "woke" forces and the MAGA opposition, what side would all the major corporations, banks, and imperialist monopolies be on? And what side was China, Cuba, Iran, North Korea, Russia, Venezuela and all the other anti-imperialist countries to be on?

The answer should be obvious. We are reminded of it on CNN every day. So, as an anti-imperialist, how can you align with the more pro-imperialist side? This, of course, doesn't mean we should become partisan fighters for Trump or defend the bad things he did as President or the racist things he has said. But if Trump is the faction that is at least in words more friendly to the anti-imperialist camp, and the faction that the imperialists themselves are most threatened by, how can you in any way justify aligning against it? If it is indeed our duty to stand with the national liberation struggles of peoples across the planet and win US workers to align with them, no talk of helping the imperialists rescue their system from Trumpism or the New Right can even be considered. To be anti-imperialists we must reject the Anti-Trump movement.

13. The Boston Trap

Our duty is to mobilize the American working class to stand with the forces of national liberation around the world, and to secure the defeat of the imperialists here in their homeland. This task does not place us in any specific place on the left to right political spectrum.

During the Cold War, it seemed that the Democrats were slightly more useful as allies. The Republicans wanted militarism, suppression of civil liberties, and the weakening of labor unions. The Republicans seemed to harness white backlash against the civil rights movement during the 1970s. The Democrats at least gave lip service to the causes of peace, free speech, and opposing racism.

Your organization, the Revolutionary Communist Party, was the largest organization in a whole trend of US politics during the 1970s called the New Communist Movement. The New Communist Movement was important because it was made up of youth who had been radicalized in the 1960s by the civil rights and peace movements, but politically matured from there to the point of becoming communists. They studied Marxism-Leninism and determined that the middle class hippie counterculture left was not where they belonged. So, various organizations including your own Revolutionary Union, precursor to the RCP, got jobs in factories, cut their hair short, and abstained from using drugs. They worked to win US industrial workers to communism.

It appears that over the course of the 1970s, the various trends of the New Communist Movement retreated from working to build an actual communist movement. By 1980 and 1981, when the so-called "Reagan Revolution" took place, it appeared that most leftist groups became focused on fighting "the right-wing" not building a base for communism among the population. Their previous orientation of breaking with the mainstream of liberals and "the left" and working to build an ideological communist group based among the workers was replaced with a defensive orientation of beating back conservatives, deemed to be fascists.

The New Communist Movement played out the way it did based on tragic historical circumstances. The US economy was starting to deteriorate but remained strong enough, with a prosperous middle class steeped in anti-communism and racism that became more pro-imperialist amid the late 70s economic downturn. China's political orientation shifted as well, and confused many people who had previously sought political direction from Beijing.

One particular episode stands out as a tragic "lesson" of the period that has been mistakenly projected onto politics right up to today. This is the Boston Busing riots. In 1974, Boston began desegregating schools, busing children to different neighborhoods in the hopes of offering equal education to Black students. The result was a string of racist attacks on school buses and violent protests from white parents.

Right-wing organizations were formed such as Restore Our Alienated Rights (ROAR) that opposed "forced busing," rallying white workers around racism. The liberals condemned the racist riots. However, Black Nationalists also opposed school busing saying they wanted Black schools for Black children. The forces defending busing were mainstream liberals and democrats, and the right-wing protests had a working class, populist anti-establishment vibe to them. Here is how your described it in your memoir: "One of the things that was extremely painful to me personally, as well as to the Party overall, was when we began to look back at our practice around the big upheaval over the school busing program that was instituted in Boston in the mid-1970s. The neighborhood in

Boston into which Black students were being bused was a bastion of segregation, including in the schools, which were essentially all-white. In these conditions, white supremacist and fascistic

In 1974, racist riots broke out in Boston against school desegregation.

sentiment was being mobilized among the white people to oppose this busing plan, but more than that to attack the Black people, the Black families, and even the Black students who were being bused in. During this period, before the Revolutionary Communist Party was formed, we in the RU had taken the position of opposing busing plans of this kind. Our approach to this was very eclectic at best. In one aspect, our thinking was similar to a number of Black nationalist forces and some progressive-minded people who opposed busing plans of this kind because these plans were part of an overall policy that allowed the schools in the Black neighborhoods to further deteriorate rather than putting more funding into and building up those schools. But, at the same time, our position on this actually represented a narrow and ultimately reformist approach which sought in a certain sense to finesse some of these intense contradictions in a kind of economist way. For example, we raised the demand for "decent and equal education," which on the one hand could be part of a correct program, but in actual circumstances objectively amounted to an avoidance of the central question of segregation. As we saw it, the ruling class was fanning antagonisms among different nationalities—and, of course, there was truth to that. But, in this situation, rather than grasping that the key to opposing that was to fight against segregation and in that context raise demands like "decent and equal education," we instead tried to maneuver our way around this by presenting a position that called for building up all the schools, and in particular strengthening the schools in the inner city. We fell into thinking that if we carried forward work in the working class around what we soon came to call the "center of gravity" of the workers' economic needs and struggles, we could get them to unite on that basis, and in that context we could get the white workers to oppose discrimination and racism. What went along with that, when it came to these busing plans, was to oppose them and instead call for decent and equal education all the way around, as if we could somehow finesse the antagonisms that were being fanned with these busing programs... And this was very painful to me personally, especially looking back on it and seeing it more clearly, because a crucial part of how I came to be a revolutionary and ultimately a communist, and of what has sustained me in that, has been a deep hatred for white supremacy and the recognition that it is built into this system and can only be abolished and uprooted through a radical, thoroughgoing transformation of society. And here's an important lesson. It is not that my hatred, or the hatred of my comrades, for white supremacy had diminished in the slightest. But when you're trying to determine how to implement a strategy to make revolution and transform all of society and how to bring forward the necessary forces to do that, you're confronted with the need to approach things differently than when you're just proceeding from your basic feelings about things... At that time the RU was putting out *Revolution* as a monthly newspaper, and I happened to be in a leadership meeting of the RU when the newspaper came out which put forward our position in opposition to this busing plan. As I recall, the headline was something like "People Must Unite To Smash Boston Busing Plan." One of the comrades who was responsible for putting out the newspaper brought the newspaper, hot off the press, to this leadership meeting. I and the others there were horrified at this headline. Because, while we did have a wrong position on this, this is not the way we felt that our position should be expressed and put forward, this was not the stand we thought should be taken, let alone blared in the headline of Revolution newspaper. We did try to move to correct this as quickly as we could, and one of the things that we did do was to make a point of searching out, uniting with and then popularizing, through our newspaper and in other ways, instances where people stood up against these white supremacist mobs, including instances where white people had stood up against them and moved to defend the Black students and others who were being attacked by these mobs. Still, our position was eclectic and essentially wrong."

To put it simply, you made a mistake. Based on support for Black nationalists who opposed busing like the Black Panthers, and a correct instinct of wanting to stand with the working class and win them to communism away from the liberals, you miscalculated. It was clearly wrong to oppose busing in the context of racist mobs attacking Black students, but your thinking in doing so wasn't completely off the mark. The article in your newspaper defending this position wrote: "Those who think that the only way to stand with Black people and other oppressed nationalities is to attack white workers as simply a bunch of racists, who think the ruling class is a friend of the oppressed, can at best only drag at the tail of the struggle, and if they continue in this path, can only end up falling over backwards completely into the camp of the ruling class."

The above sentences are accurate. The ruling class are not defenders of the oppressed. Attacking white workers as racists is not the correct approach for building up anti-imperialism and solidarity. However, in the aftermath of this mistaken position on busing, your organization was roundly condemned by other leftist groups. After your organization apologized for its mistaken position, you became the negative example, the whipping boy, in the rhetoric of aligning leftists with the democrats. The Workers World Party still harps on about events in Boston in 1974 as proof of their supposed higher caliber as anti-racists in comparison to you and the October League. *Heavy Radicals* narrates: "the RU's position was ridiculed widely on the left, and inside its own ranks it created serious dissension… The political fallout would have lasting consequences for the RU in terms of loss of prestige if not legitimacy in certain quarters."

I have come to call this "The Boston Trap" because, in our time, the orientation that one should never align with any movement that is decried as "right-wing" is completely mistaken. One simply cannot equate every political movement or cause that is opposed by the Biden-aligned "woke" left as being the equivalent of racist mobs in Boston during the 1970s.

Opposing the power of Big Pharma and the lack of transparency around the vaccine is something many working people are doing, and should be embraced for. Opposing the escalation to war with Russia and China, and the flow of weapons to Ukraine is a good thing. Opposing tech censorship, questioning mainstream media, are all legit things that millions of working people do and earn the label of "right-wing" from the establishment.

Many of the things believed by working class Americans, both white and Black, who are labeled as "right-wing extremists" by US media, are completely legitimate and progressive. It seems that since 1974 your organization has over-corrected. You have forgotten the wisdom of what you wrote in your editorial defending a mistaken position. To dismiss Trump's supporters and the millions who voted for him out of anger at the wars and impoverishment of their communities as "a bunch of racists," to rally behind Joe Biden and the ruling elite as a "defenders of the oppressed" has led to millions of so-called communists and socialists "falling over backwards completely into the camp of the ruling class."

One passage from your autobiography is particularly painful for me to read. In it you describe a kind of revelation you had at a Jimmy Buffet concert: "...as the struggle with these Mensheviks was developing and sharpening up a bit, after the revisionist coup in China, I went to a Jimmy Buffet concert. I had listened to some Jimmy Buffet songs because Jimmy Buffet sort of had one foot in youth culture and one foot in the country western culture. He came to Chicago and he had his band which was called the Coral Reefer

Band; and of course reefer was a play on words—on the one hand it referred to the Caribbean influences in his music but then it was also… reefer. And at this Jimmy Buffet concert there was a lot of reefer; there were a lot of jokes from the stage from Jimmy Buffet and the band about reefer and a lot of people in the audience were smoking reefer. In the audience there were a lot of youth from the middle class, but there were also a lot of young white proletarians there, who were into all of this. And this might seem odd, but even in the form of all this talk about reefer, and the people joking about it, there was a certain rebellious edge, and it made me think: we've gotten into tailing after more intermediate sections of the workers, or even the more backward among the white workers. There are workers, including among the white youth, who are more alienated and rebellious than many of the more stable and more conservative tending workers among whom we had been focusing much of our work. It is right to have a strategic orientation toward winning as many as possible among the more intermediate workers, and even more backward workers, to socialism, but this should not be our main focus. In a way, this Jimmy Buffet concert, while in and of itself a small thing, was part of provoking questions in my mind politically and ideologically."

Starting in the late 1970s your organization shifted away from trying to win over the bulk of the working class. Your focus shifted to low-income Black workers in urban centers, middle class radicals and "edgy youth." This orientation makes no sense in our time.

A new hit country song among Trump supporters, *Rich Men North of Richmond* contains the lyrics: "I've been sellin' my soul, workin' all day/Overtime hours for bullshit pay/So I can sit out here and waste my life away/Drag back home and drown my troubles away…Livin' in the new world/With an old soul/These rich men north of Richmond, Lord knows they all/Just wanna have total control/Wanna know what you think, wanna know what you do/And they don't think you know, but I know that you do/'Cause your dollar ain't shit and it's taxed to no end/'Cause of rich men north of Richmond/I wish politicians would look out for miners/And not just minors on an island somewhere/Lord, we got folks in the street, ain't got nothin' to eat."

Class consciousness is everywhere among the American working class. They are angry at the wars, the ultra-rich and their puppet politicians, and the political system that seems rigged against them. Where do you expect the growing outrage and anger to be redirected if it is not transformed into revolutionary politics? Aligning with the liberal pro-war establishment against an increasingly impoverished angry working class is a tactical blunder that is making your politics worse each day. Those of us who are anti-imperialists and advocate the creation of a socialist society must find a way to win them over. If there has ever been a time when this was an urgent necessity, it is now.

14. They used you in 1979

As I said before, there is nothing wrong with aligning with one faction of the ruling class against another. But what disturbs me as I look over your history as a revolutionary, is that it seems very likely that rather than knowingly strategically joining one faction of the ruling class against another, you have been, for lack of better words, "used."

The intelligence apparatus and competing factions within the American deep state have infiltrated your organization or found ways of manipulating it into unconsciously doing its bidding. The most blatant example I can think of is the 1979 protest at the White House you organized under the slogan "Death to Deng Xiaoping."

After Mao Zedong died in 1976, the new leadership in China had arrested the Gang of Four and launched a "reform and opening up." New policies allowing free market zones and elements of capitalism were being implemented. You considered this proof that China had "restored capitalism" and your organization underwent a pretty serious division in relation to this issue.

In the aftermath of a devastating split in which your mentor Leibel Bergman and yourself were on opposite sides, your organization decided to protest Deng Xiaoping's visit to Jimmy Carter at the White House, which was part of the United States and China establishing diplomatic relations.

China had been aligning with the United States on geopolitical issues since 1968. China denounced the Soviet Union for sending its forces to Czechoslovakia and crushing the CIA-backed "Prague Spring." China aligned with US-backed anti-communists in Angola and provided them military support the following year. China began talking about "Soviet Social Imperialism" and declaring that the Soviet Union was not only "revisionist" and abandoning genuinely Marxist-Leninist policies, but had in fact become a capitalist-imperialist empire. China went as far as saying the USSR was "the main danger" and not the United States.

Nixon visited China in 1972, despite many within his own party opposing it. The John Birch Society and other hard right-wing organizations put up billboards across the country accusing China of being responsible for the flow of heroin and opposing Nixon's visit. One of the primary voices supporting Nixon's visit to China was David Rockefeller, the heir of one of the wealthiest oil-banking dynasties in the country.

As the 1970s proceeded, following Nixon's ouster, the Rockefeller-Kissinger policy of the US getting closer to China proceeded. George H.W. Bush was sent to China where he directed the US Liaison Office in Beijing from 1974 to 1975. Finally, in 1979, the Carter administration was moving forward with establishing full diplomatic relations. The US withdrew its recognition from the supposed "Republic of China" on Taiwan, and recognized the Communist Party-led government on the mainland.

The hard right-wing opposed this move, seeing China as a communist government that was untrustworthy. The 2014 book, written by two academics, Aaron Leonard and Connor Gallagher,

Heavy Radicals: The FBI's Secret War on America's Maoists, cites declassified government documents revealing that the Revolutionary Communist Party was crawling with informants and government agents at this time.

One of the main vehicles through which the RCP was infiltrated was an organization called Western Goals. The group was a domestic private intelligence service started by Congressman Larry Mcdonald. The organization provided training and funding for members of the John Birch Society and the World Anti-Communist League to join Communist organizations, gather information and manipulate them from the inside. Western Goals provided information to the FBI and was considered useful by the pro-Reagan, anti-Carter wing of the American intelligence apparatus. John Rees was one of the main leaders of Western Goals, and his wife Sheila Rees infiltrated the RCP in

Washington DC. Sheila used her maiden name, and operating as Sheila O'connor she worked at the National Lawyers Guild office and eventually became a long term informant within the RCP. Eventually, as her husband's *Information Digest* became the subject of investigations by the New York State Legislature, she was forced to stop operating as an FBI informant due to fear of being subpoenaed. Western Goals eventually dissolved in 1986 after its role in the Iran-Contra scandal became public.

It is clear that Western Goals, a private intelligence organization that was tied to political forces that opposed normalizing relations with China had sent its forces into the RCP. And in this context, your organization formed a "Committee for a Fitting Welcome" for Deng Xiaoping when he visited the White House.

The Washington Post described how you had a press conference at a hotel in the US capital and basically took credit for attacking the embassy: "The group, called the Revolutionary Communist Party (USA) Committee for a Fitting Welcome, held a press conference at the Executive House Motor Hotel yesterday to announce its goals and tactics. While reporters served themselves from an elegant coffee urn and ate danish pastries arrayed on linen-covered tables, members of the RCP (USA) stood in front of posters of Mao Tse-tung, Karl Marx and Lenin denouncing Teng as a "posturing bootlicker and sawed-off pimp" who has sold out to the capitalists. "We are working for civil war," said Bob Avakian, central committee chairman of the PRC (USA). "The kind of thing that happened at the embassy yesterday is an example of a 'fitting welcome'... A warning has been issued and a call has been made." (Washington Post, Jan. 26th, 1979)

When Deng Xiaoping did arrive in DC, your organization continued with its work intended to undermine US-China relations. An article from *The Washington Post*, published January 30th, 1979 describes how "two RCP activists with press credentials briefly disrupted the welcoming ceremonies on the south lawn yesterday morning when they began shouting anti-Teng slogans. They were quickly hustled away by Secret Service agents and charged with disorderly conduct. The two -- identified by Secret Service as Keith Scott Kozimoto, 28, of New York, and Sonia J Ransom, also known as Jean Goldberg, 26, of Seattle -- had been admitted to the White House grounds with temporary press passes. A Secret Service spokesman said both had credentials for The

Worker newspaper which is published by the Revolutionary Communist Party."

The two individuals wrote their own account of this action later, describing how they acquired passes to get onto the White House grounds. The account published in the Revolutionary Communist Party's press and now available on the Marxist Internet Archive tells the following: "We got in line behind others in the press, all with our green and white credentials on chains around our necks. I was anxious to get in and get started. The day before at Andrews Air Force Base we had gone to test the water and see if we could make it in. We met a lot of other members of the press who are interested in the Workers Press Service, and what it is. In another situation, I would have gone into depth, but yesterday I tried to play it cool. Didn't want to get thrown out before the big day. "We cover news of interest to workers from the point of view of the working class," and invariably, they would reply, "Oh, are you connected with the people who attacked the Chinese mission?" A few reporters wanted to know our differences with the *Daily Worker* and how we viewed the current regime, "Are you Maoists?" they asked. "Well, yes," we answered, hoping the discussion would end. In addition, some of the reporters from a reactionary Chinatown paper recognized Keith. "I hope we get in," I thought. "I hope we didn't blow it yesterday." "Press credentials and one piece of photo I.D.," said the Secret Service man at the gate. I was wearing my credentials for the trip, so I pulled out one other piece of I.D. I felt the Red Book next to my skin and thought of the Traitor Teng leaflets in an envelope in my purse. I was ready. Go right in, he said. We did. We were in. The first hurdle was crossed."

This account obviously raises some questions. As a reporter who has worked in Washington DC, I can attest as to how difficult it is to get into events on the White House grounds. Perhaps it was easier in the past, but it is doubtful that open Communists would be allowed to do so, especially those from an organization that had just attacked and dramatically vandalized the newly opened Chinese embassy days beforehand.

At the height of the Cold War, when Communism was designated as the national enemy ideology, why would the US Air Force and Secret Service grant press credentials to open communists. It appears that Kozimoto and Ransom were not even deceptive in acquiring them, but openly engaging the other reporters lining up to apply for admission to White House grounds about being Communists. This indicates that the two had some kind of confirmation that they would be allowed to get into the White House and do what they did. Who told the two RCP activists they should apply for credentials? Who let them know it was safe to apply honestly as Communists?

The account goes on: "Walking down the path to the White House, my first thought was, how clean it is, so white. Nothing else looks like that in D.C. The poster the Chinese made in the 1960s showing the Black liberation struggle storming and burning the Capitol flashed through my mind. We won't accomplish that, today, I thought, but it will be a taste of what's to come. The press was everywhere, outside waiting, inside the White House press room."

Is this the language that someone who has just been arrested and is facing criminal charges for infiltrating White House grounds and disrupting proceedings to harass a foreign head of state would use when narrating their activities? The article was published in February of 1979, just shortly after the incident. The writer seems to be confessing to left-adventurist terrorist ideation, something that could easily be used against them in court proceedings. The language is not only incriminating and unwise, it is inconsistent with how Marxist-Leninist revolutionaries generally speak. Communists talk about a popular revolution of the working class, not left-adventurism and violent coup d'etats. The language almost sounds like a comic book caricature of a communist villian's stream of consciousness i.e. "darn, we couldn't burn and destroy and loot the country today… but at least I could threaten a foreign head of state and make a scene!" The author clearly had no fear of legal consequences for infiltrating the White House grounds and threatening a foreign head of state.

The account continues: "Carter and Teng came back to the platform. I tried to move to the front. "When should I break in," I thought. I wanted to wait for Teng, but I wasn't positive that he was going to speak. Carter stepped forward to the podium. "On behalf of the American people, I want to welcome you." You don't speak for the American people, I thought. "Our peoples have had a long history of friendship marred by only 30 years."...Like many before me, I raised the Red Book high. I knew Teng would know what it was. I wonder if he thought he'd seen the last of it. That bastard! I wish we could give him what he really deserves. ...Knowing millions worldwide would stand with my words, I shouted as loud as I could, "The Revolutionary Communist Party says Down with Teng Hsiao-ping!" Carter and I looked right into each other's eyes. He started to talk louder. I yelled, "The Revolutionary Communist Party says

Long Live Mao Tse Tung!" I can't remember exactly when the secret service agent grabbed me. They must have been shocked that after all their

In 1979, the RCP organized a series of provocative demonstrations against Deng Xiaoping. Two RCP activists penetrated White House grounds.

tightened security we made it into their impenetrable fortress. These members of the palace guard were all decked out in black uniforms, gold braid and white shirts. They looked like little tin soldiers. They grabbed both my arms and tried to push down my head. When I got outside the press corral, as they were dragging me out, I somehow was able to face Jimmy Carter again, and I yelled, "Teng, you murderer! You may have killed tens of thousands of revolutionaries, you may be kissing the boots of U.S. imperialism, but you will never stop revolution. The Chinese people will overthrow you once again." Then they started pushing me harder and faster. All the secret service, Teng and Carter breathed a sigh of relief. I was listening intensely, since I knew it was just the beginning."

This provocative act of infiltrating the White House grounds and creating an incident in front of international media, grabbing both Deng Xiaoping and Jimmy Carter's attention was clearly allowed to happen. Forces that did not want the improvement of US-China relations, for very different reasons than you and your comrades, were using you as pawns. Western Goals, which had a tight relationship with the FBI, used your organization to further its own right-wing agenda.

That night your organization is reported to have engaged in an extremely provocative demonstration. This is the account published in *The Washington Post*: "Suddenly, as they approached the park from the east along Pennsylvania Avenue, they broke into a run, shouting "Death, Death to Teng Hsiao-ping" and began hurling bottles, poles, lighted road flares, and hundreds of nails, heavy washers and fishing sinkers at both D.C. and U.S. Park Police gathered near the park. Police, apparently caught off guard, quickly recovered and with reinforcements charged into the crowd, swinging their clubs wildly. Many demonstrators swung back with their improvised clubs. A young woman, blood coming from her nose and mouth, was taken away on a stretcher. Police and local hospitals reported at least 38 demonstrators were treated and released for bruises and head lacerations. At least 13 police officers were injured, including one Park officer who was thrown from his horse. Another officer suffered a broken finger, Park Police said. The RCP, which claimed responsibility for vandalizing the new People's Republic of China embassy here last week, said yesterday they plan more unspecified "actions" while Teng is in town. The Chinese leader is scheduled to leave Washington early Thursday."

An interesting event happened later the same year. In August of 1979, the *Los Angeles Times* misquoted you as threatening Jimmy Carter. It was a misrepresentation of your words, and you filed legal action immediately. The *LA Times* published a retraction. The false reporting of your words became the basis of a prolonged secret-service investigation into you and your organization.

It appears that a wing of the deep state that opposed Carter's moves to establish friendly relations with China was using you and your organization, not just to threaten Deng Xiaoping but to intimidate Jimmy Carter. You were being held up in false media reporting as a potential Lee Harvey Oswald, hinting to Carter that he could suffer the same fate as John F. Kennedy.

In November of 1979, when US diplomats were being held as hostages in Iran, your organization took on the task for itself of going to patriotic anti-Iran rallies, burning US flags, and provoking violent attacks from the right-wing crowds. You announced "Its not our fucking embassy, its not even our fucking country! We just live here" at a rally, and as part of the May Day Brigades your members proceeded to attend right-wing anti-Iran protests and get beaten up.

These anti-Iran protests that accused Carter of being soft, set the stage for Ronald Reagan to win the 1980 election in a landslide. Carter's SALT treaty with the Soviet Union had been condemned by 170 retired Generals and Admirals in a *New York Times* ad in January of 1979. Carter's "crisis of confidence" aka malaise speech, further antagonized these forces. The military and the FBI were mobilizing against Jimmy Carter and the soft-power oriented wing of the establishment. In the narrative they were constructing and staged rallies they were putting on across the country, you were the "heel" to use professional wrestling lingo. You were the caricature of foul mouthed, flag burning,

America-hating communists to rile up the right-wing crowds and set the stage for the Reagan revolution.

I sincerely doubt this is a role your organization intentionally took on for itself. I think you genuinely loathed Deng Xiaoping and genuinely supported the Islamic Revolution of Iran. But it appears the hard militaristic right-wing, through its covert methods, used you for a very different agenda. Western Goals had inserted itself deeply into your organization as had a number of other government informants. *Heavy Radicals* goes into great detail about this.

15. French Imperialism & Covert Manipulation

After the chaotic events of 1979 and 1980, you fled to Paris. You made a big point of applying for political exile status. You describe the process this way: "The experience of applying for political refugee status in France, in 1981, was very interesting and revealing, and very intense. I didn't actually apply directly to the French government. The way the process worked was that you went to the UN High Commission on Refugees, which was in Paris, and you applied there for political refugee status. And if that commission of the UN granted you political refugee status, then the French government was supposed to grant you the rights that went with that, including the right to remain and be able to live and work in France. When I went with my lawyer to the office of the UN High Commission in Paris, we went from one desk to another in the office with my application for political refugee status, and we were turned away at each one. They kept demanding to know, "Where are you exiled from?" When I would answer, "the United States," I would be told, "We don't have a desk for the United States or North America, because the United States is a democratic country." In effect they were telling me— and finally one person in the office told me explicitly—that I couldn't even file my application for political

The Revolutionary Communist Party was heavily involved in the protests that prevented the execution of Mumia Abu Jamal in 1995.

refugee status because I came from the United States and there is no political repression in the United States. So here I am, arguing with the people in this UN Commission office about the real nature of U.S. society: how Black people and others are shot down and murdered by the police in the hundreds every year, how political demonstrations are attacked, such as the one that I took part in against Deng Xiaoping as well many other demonstrations against the Vietnam War and the protests that took place in the course of the civil rights and Black liberation movement, and so on. I kept exposing these things, and they just kept turning me away, sending me from one desk to another, and refusing to even accept my application to start the process…Our documents and evidentiary material included many things relating to the case that had arisen out of the attack on the demonstration against Deng Xiaoping, as well as many other examples of political repression directed against the Party and myself in particular. We had hundreds and hundreds of pages of documentation that we eventually submitted to the Commission—even though, as it turned out, they refused to read almost all of it."

You did not receive political exile status from the French government. Your application was denied. Yet, you remained in the country. The legality of your residence in France from 1982 to 2003 is not explained anywhere in your memoir or on the website of your organization. If not as a political exile, you must have gotten some kind of visa from the French government, especially if you made them highly aware of your presence in the country beforehand by applying for exile status.

You were not the only 1960s radical to have fled the United States for France. Your friend and co-worker from *Ramparts*, Black Panther leader

Eldridge Cleaver lived in Paris for a time before becoming a born-again Christian and returning to the United States in 1975. While leaving out the details of how you remained in France, you admit that you were introduced into some kind of association of leftist expats from various countries who had set up shop in Paris. You write: "I met people from countries in Latin America and elsewhere where the U.S. had pulled off coups and installed brutal dictatorships that tormented and tortured, and brutalized and murdered thousands and thousands of people. I talked to many Chilean refugees, for example, who gave vivid accounts of this. **A number of people I met, including refugees from other countries who had been in France for a while, helped me learn the ropes, as they say, and in various ways were supportive.** And there had also been some political work done, in France and other parts of Europe, around the

LETTER TO BOB AVAKIAN

Mao Tsetung Defendants case, so that had laid the groundwork for some people to understand why I had to go into exile. All in all, **I found a great deal of sympathy and support of various kinds** when I arrived in Paris." (Emphasis C.M.)

It is interesting that the leader of an obscure political party in the United States could go to a completely foreign country and get "a great deal of sympathy and support of various kinds." It is also interesting that many Communists from around the world had also found their way to the capital of a major imperialist country. It is worth noting that France, while being a member of NATO with its forces deployed across Africa, has a history of being at odds with the US and British imperialists.

On the 7th of June 1981, Israel murdered a French citizen with the backing of the United States. France was helping Iraq to develop peaceful nuclear energy. Israel launched "Operation Opera" also known as "Operation Babylon" destroying the Iraqi nuclear facility. Ten Iraqi soldiers were killed, along with a French civilian nuclear power technician. The United States had urged France to stop helping Iraq develop nuclear energy, but France had refused.

In 1981, around the same time you fled to Paris, another left-wing activist named Ira Einhorn also defected to France. Ira Einhorn was an environmentalist who had many times claimed to be the founder of Earth Day. He went by his hippie moniker 'Unicorn' and was the master of ceremonies at the Philadelphia Earth Day celebration in 1970. He was a well known figure in leftist and activist circles in Philadelphia before his girlfriend's body was found, partially mummified in his apartment and he was charged with murder. Many leftists and community activists pressured the court to grant him bail, and a member of the ultra-rich Canadian Bronfman family put up the cash. Right before his trial was to begin, Ira Einhorn, dubbed "The Unicorn Killer" disappeared.

Einhorn was discovered living in rural France in 1997 where he had lived for over a decade under the name "Eugène Mallon." Einhorn was able to fight his extradition until 2001. All kinds of efforts were made by the French government to delay and deny extradition. The French government finally agreed to extradite him in 2001 only after a special law was passed in Pennsylvania enabling the French government to receive assurance that he would not receive the death penalty.

When Einhorn went on trial in 2002, he argued that his girlfriend had in fact been killed by the CIA and that he had collected evidence of their mind control programs. Einhorn read all kinds of testimony about covert CIA operations and technology and his direct cooperation and involvement in their activities into the record at his trial. Einhorn was found guilty and spent the rest of his life in prison, dying in 2022 during the COVID-19 pandemic.

Einhorn clearly had help leaving the United States while under indictment for murder and facing the death penalty. Einhorn also had help getting to France and living under a false name for well over a decade. Einhorn also had overwhelming sympathy from the French legal system in that his extradition was delayed for so long and such stringent demands were placed on the US state of Pennsylvania in order to secure it.

When it comes to the use of the death penalty in the US State of Pennsylvania and prominent court cases in the US city of Philadelphia, it is certainly interesting that one of the criminal cases

LETTER TO BOB AVAKIAN

your organization was essential in determining the outcome of was that of Mumia Abu Jamal.

Mumia is a former Black Panther and radio journalist from Philadelphia who was convicted in 1982, the same year you went into exile, of murdering a police officer. As his execution became imminent, first only the Spartacist League, but eventually many other Marxist and Leftist groups spoke up on his behalf. Your organization and its youth wing 'Refuse and Resist' became the most visible and outspoken supporters of Mumia in the late 1980s and throughout the 90s.

When Mumia's death warrant was signed in 1995 by the Governor of Pennsylvania, voices across the planet spoke out. The Pope denounced the planned execution. Buses of Mennonites and religious pacifists piled into Philadelphia. Communists, Anarchists, Environmentalists, Amnesty International and many different organizations put their energy and resources into stopping the execution.

C. Clark Kissinger, a leader of the Revolutionary Communist Party, was one of the most outspoken and pivotal organizers who helped successfully prevent Mumia Abu Jamal's execution in 1995. The band "Rage Against The Machine" highlighted Mumia's case, and featured the organization "Refuse and Resist" started by Revolutionary Communist Party members on the liner notes of the widely sold album "The Battle of Los Angeles."

I believe Mumia Abu Jamal is innocent, and I think stopping his execution was a great thing. I am glad your organization did so much to save Mumia's life and I am glad that you were able to muster so much passion and dedication among your members toward this end. I hope someday Mumia can be released from prison.

But one thing must be pointed out. A lot of the opposition to Mumia Abu Jamal's execution came from France with 25 cities, including Paris, declaring Mumia Abu Jamal to be an honorary citizen. In October of 2006, Paris even named a street "Rue Mumia Abu Jamal" in his honor. When Paris granted citizenship to Mumia in 2003, a ceremony was held in City Hall where Mayor Bertrand Delanoe pumped his fist and chanted "Mumia is a Parisian! Mumia is a Parisian!" Dr. Angela Davis accepted the certificate of citizenship on his behalf.

I know for a fact that much of the fundraising in support of pro-Mumia activism by the International Action Center, an activist group dominated by the Workers World Party and led by the late former US Attorney General Ramsey Clark was also done in France. Larry Holmes traveled throughout France during the 1990s, fundraising for Mumia's legal defense and his own organization in different regions.

It should be noted that the French Communist Party denounced the Soviet Union in 1978 and became "Euro-Communists." The French Communist Party has significant representation in the French government with 12 seats in the National Assembly and 14 in the Senate. The French Communist Party openly supported the NATO-led bombing of Libya in 2011 and most other military interventions carried out by the Atlanticist coalition. The French Communist Party was a major voice supporting the US-led efforts to topple the Syrian Arab Republic.

Unlike your organization in the United States, the French Communist Party, which supported Mumia Abu Jamal, is more or less a wing of the government and operates in an unspoken alliance with its intelligence services, echoing support for

French foreign policy. The French Communist Party's position on the war in Ukraine is more or less identical to that of your organization. The organization opposes escalation and more weapons to Kiev, but also denounces Russia as being the aggressor. The pages of *L'humanite* repeat slanders against the Russian government and take at face value reports of alleged atrocities against Ukrainian civilians.

You returned to the United States in 2003, just before George W. Bush was re-elected in a highly contested Presidential race. When you returned you held two events with RCP members, one on the west coast and the other on the east coast and released them as a DVD, combining footage of the two events, entitled "Revolution: Why It's Necessary, Why It's Possible, What It's All About."

The moment of your return was a pivotal moment of division between the United States and

France. France had a much better relationship with Iraq than the USA and Britain did, importing a lot of its oil. French President Jacques Chirac had opposed the US invasion of Iraq before the world. In response, the US congressional cafeteria renamed French fries "freedom fries." Bush's supporters whipped up a campaign against France as a country that had betrayed America. FOX news even played up the notion that Bush's Democratic rival in the 2004 election was sympathetic to the supposedly back-stabbing French, repeating the phrase "John Kerry is French" in their broadcasts.

France's opposition to the Bush administration and its unilateral invasion of Iraq was hardly restrained. Michael Moore's documentary film *Fahrenheit 9/11,* demonizing US President George Bush, debuted at the Cannes Film Festival in 2004 and won the *Palme d'Or*, the highest award of the year. The film received a standing ovation at its conclusion that went on for hours. Despite being so widely celebrated in France, Disney launched a legal battle attempting to prevent its distribution to theaters in the United States.

British playwright Harold Pinter was awarded the Nobel Prize for Literature in 2005, and used the occasion of the award ceremony to give a lengthy speech denouncing the Bush administration. He received the French *Légion d'honneur* award in 2007. At the time, the RCP devoted a large amount of space in its publications to highlighting Pinter's work and remarks.

We can all recall how during Barack Obama's 2008 Presidential campaign he went to Berlin to speak to crowds of Europeans, hoping to restore the relationship the Bush administration had damaged with NATO rivals.

In intelligence circles an individual or organization is considered an "asset," not when they willingly join in cahoots with some covert entity, but when their behavior is predictable and can be effectively manipulated. While Hollywood presents the intelligence world as one of James Bond adventurers, assassinations, bombings and exploding cars, much of what the intelligence services of the world focus on is crafting public opinion. We know it is the covert work of the CIA that put the US at the center of the computer revolution. Furthermore, we know that the CIA meddled in the world of arts and culture with its Congress for Cultural Freedom program, promoting Jackson Pollack in opposition to socialist realism, and promoting experimental music.

It appears that much of the work of your organization since your arrival in France during the early 80s lines up with the agenda of entities within the French state and among the French ruling class in their rivalry with American imperialism. This does not mean the work you have done is bad. Opposing the invasion of Iraq, working in support of Mumia Abu Jamal, calling for the impeachment of George W. Bush, are all noble deeds even if the French imperialists would support them in their rivalry with the Americans.

However, your neutral position on Ukraine that repeats anti-Russian talking points, your opposition to the existing socialist countries, all while presenting them as a kind of welfare state alternative to your Jacobin vision of ultra-democracy "Liberte, Egalite, Fraternite," also lines up with what many in the French ruling class might approve of, or at the very least, be willing to stomach in exchange for seeing other goals met.

While American intelligence organizations, despite their often eccentric methods of covert manipulation, are steeped in decades of anti-communist orientation, the French intelligence services are not. When it comes to handling revolutionary intellectuals like yourself, men from the middle class who boil with anger at the oppressive order, sympathize with third world liberation movements and victims of racism, and compose screeds about their unique utopian visions, the French have plenty of experience. France is crawling with men similar to yourself who dabble in philosophy, lead small organizations that call themselves "revolutionary," and consider themselves to be a renaissance man of one kind or another.

I have no direct information about the circumstances of your time in exile and the "friends" you may have made, the support that may have been offered to you, the nudging you may have received to speak on certain topics, the redlines you may have been given on certain issues in exchange for donations, publicity or other favors. But there seems to be no question that the work of your organization has lined up directly with the covert operations and goals of the French imperialist state, most especially when it is at odds with the United States.

While you seem to have no loyalty to the anti-imperialist camp centered around Russia and China, your organization clings like superglue to liberal, pro-NATO "woke" bourgeoisie. You see defending them against Donald Trump and the right-wing opposition as your top priority, so much so that you dropped your longstanding anti-electoral position in 2020 in order to urge your members to vote for Joe Biden.

John Bolton recently declared that if Trump is re-elected as President of the United States, NATO will be abolished. I strongly urge you to consider how your organization may have been pushed into a corner, and manipulated by forces who are doing all they can to make sure this does not happen.

Seeing NATO abolished would be a great thing. It would weaken and divide the imperialist camp. It would strengthen the forces of resistance around the world that have enabled people in places like Africa and South America to seek economic development and break the chains of poverty.

In the lead up to the First World War, Leon Trotsky agitated for a "United States of Europe." Lenin denounced this in his famous essay "Imperialism and the Split in Socialism." He said unity among the imperialists was not desirable, and called for a full break with the opportunist socialists who seemed to have attached themselves to the imperialist bourgeoisie, despite speaking in the name of Marxism. Lenin described the methods through which imperialists were duped into being allies of one imperialist state or another:

"the political institutions of modern capitalism—press, parliament associations, congresses etc.—have created *political* privileges and sops for the respectful, meek, reformist and patriotic office employees and workers, corresponding to the economic privileges and sops. Lucrative an soft jobs in the government or on the war industries committees, in parliament and on diverse committees, on the editorial staffs of "respectable", legally published newspapers or on the management councils of no less respectable and "bourgeois law-abiding" trade unions—this is the bait by which the imperialist bourgeoisie attracts and rewards the representatives and supporters of the "bourgeois labor parties."

It is pretty clear that "woke" politics has been cultivated with the same kind of bribery - funding for academic research, tenured positions on the University staff, highlighting in the bourgeois press for your "anti-fascist" youtube videos, expansion of your social media platform. The "woke" left has been cultivated much with the same methods that the social-imperialist left, "social-democrats" and "Marxists" that led workers off to their deaths, was cultivated in the early 20th century.

Leon Trotsky's agitating for the United States of Europe, rooted in his theory of permanent revolution, is most likely a result of the covert support he received from German intelligence officer, arms dealer, and "socialist" Alexander Parvus. Trotsky's calls for creating some kind of European Union were in the interests of German imperialism. However, let us not forget that Alexander Parvus also helped Lenin to return to Russia from Switzerland and deliver his April Theses, preparing the Bolsheviks to take power just months later. Alliances with factions among the imperialist bourgeoisie are not inherently wrong.

But they should be carried out consciously and strategically.

For whatever reason, you and your organization are in an alliance with the Biden faction, the liberal "woke" imperialists, in their efforts to suppress the populism and dissent of the New Right. I think you are on the wrong side.

16. Old and New Atheism

One of the biggest tactical blunders I observed your organization make started around 2006 but culminated in the release of your book *Away With All Gods!* in 2008. You led your organization to launch a campaign of tailism, aimed at the New Atheist movement. As the *New York Times*, CNN, and other mainstream media outlets in the United States were highlighting the work of Richard Dawkins, Sam Harris and Christopher Hitchens, you threw your hat into the ring hoping to recruit some cynical anti-Christians and sell some books yourself.

You completely miscalculated and misunderstood the nature of the new atheist movement. The term "atheist" was first used in French (athée) in 1566, and came into widespread use during the French Revolution and the following upheavals of the 1790s. The term refers to those who deny or do not accept the existence of a deity. When the French "atheists" were converting Catholic cathedrals into Temples of Reason and executing priests, they did so in rebellion against an unjust feudal order that claimed divine right. The King claimed to be appointed by God to rule over the country as a "natural superior."

Atheism was associated with mass revolutionary movements of peasants and workers, revolting against reactionary structures that oppressed them and justified their crimes by invoking religion. Karl Marx viewed religion as "the heart of a heartless world, the soul of soulless conditions." Like others from the revolutionary intelligentsia which was widespread in Europe at

The primary voice of the New Atheist movement is Richard Dawkins, an advocate of eugenics and social Darwinism.

the time, he opposed religion and favored science and reason as an alternative.

But the "New Atheists" that arose in the 21st Century are of a completely different character. Richard Dawkins, one of the most famous among them, became prominent for writing a sociobiological and social-Darwinist screed defending inequality called "The Selfish Gene." The text attempts to explain human behavior by looking at animals. The text is celebrated by the elitist malthusian circles in Britain, who have used social-Darwinism and eugenics to justify their imperialist crimes for generations.

While the atheists of the past celebrated human intelligence and achievement and accused religion of suppressing the rational nature of humanity, the New Atheists do the opposite. They oppose religion because it views human beings as separate from animals, and they interpret human behavior as being fundamentally no different than that of animals. While the old atheists saw humanity uniquely intelligent and beautiful, the new atheists view humanity with utter contempt.

The old atheists ranted against the crimes of colonialism and imperialism, often justified with religious rhetoric. The new atheists attack religion as primitive, and specifically attack the third world for being "backward" in its religious nature. The new atheists single out Islam for the most extreme demonization, and often make blatantly pro-Israel statements, justifying the crimes of "civilized" and "secular" Israel against the "theocratic" Palestinian Muslims.

The New Atheist movement has nothing to do with Marxism. The New Atheist movement is a repackaging of the ideas of Friedrich Nietschze, Leo Strauss and Ayn Rand. It is post-modern philosophical irrationalism as identified by

Hungarian Marxist Georg Lucaks in his groundbreaking text *The Destruction of Reason*. The New Atheist says that right and wrong do not exist, the nature of the universe is chaos rather than order, human beings are just another animal with no special unique quality of intelligence or creativity, and that historical progress is a delusion.

The New Atheist tends to decry not just religion, but all attempts to explain the nature of reality in a coherent or "totalistic" way. It views religion as just another brand of ideology and morality, and sees the only ethical task as being the deconstruction of such world views.

New Atheism was being promoted in 2006 and 2008 as a push-back against the Neoconservatives who ran the United States. The Bush administration had driven oil prices up, alienated Europe and US allies in the Muslim world, and allowed Bolivarian Socialism, the Islamic Republic of Iran and Russia to become stronger. The Neoconservatives were quickly replaced with Barack Hussein Obama and the Hillary Clinton State Department who fomented the Arab Spring and tried to reassert US dominance over the world.

Many of the New Atheists have evolved into blatant racists and white supremacists. Richard Dawkins and Sam Harris have both promoted eugenics and racial pseudoscience. Many of the young white men who became followers of Richard Spencer and the alt-right were young New Atheists who had broken with the evangelical conservatism of their families as teenagers. As this generation of young men from conservative backgrounds became alienated by the "social justice warriors" that dominate the internet, this "pipeline" led them to white supremacy. Much has been written about this trajectory from New Atheism to white supremacy.

Atheism of the non-communist, but rather philosophical irrationalist variety can be found everywhere among the ruling class. Stacy Abrams and Paul Ryan both cite Ayn Rand's book *Atlas Shrugged* as their greatest source of inspiration. The belief that "might makes right" and that morality is a "tool of the weak " is the unofficial religion of Wall Street, Capitol Hill and Harvard University. It is churned out everywhere free market neoliberal economics can be found. From the business department of community colleges to cell blocks of American prisons, books by Ayn Rand who called Christianity "the guilt peddling Jesus industry" are everywhere.

You confused this new brand of pro-capitalist, anti-human demagogy with your own, strict Marxist materialism. It is worth noting that Friedrich Engels observed the unhealthy atheism of middle class intellectuals in 1874 when observing the Blanquist exile community in London, those who had fled from Paris after the defeat of the Commune. He wrote: "The point with them is, then, to be more radical in the matter of atheism than all others. Fortunately it requires no great heroism to be an atheist nowadays. Atheism is practically accepted by the European working men's parties…In order to show that they are the most radical, God is abolished by them by decree… And this demand for a transformation of people into atheists by order of the star chamber is signed by two members of the Commune, who had opportunity enough to learn in the first place, that a multitude of things may be ordered on paper without being carried out, and in the second place, that persecutions are the best means of promoting disliked convictions. So much is certain, that the only service, which may still be rendered to God today, is that of declaring atheism an article of faith to be enforced and of outdoing even Bismarck's anti-Catholic laws by forbidding religion altogether."

17. "inspired by their belief in God"

The Communist world has largely moved away from the strict dialectical materialist perspective. Fidel Castro described himself as a Christian in his final years, and had lengthy meetings with both Catholic and Orthodox clergy. Today, religion flourishes in Cuba, not just Catholicism and Protestantism, but also African Santeria and indigenous religious practices.

The slogan of the ruling Marxist party of Nicaragua is "Christianity, Socialism and Solidarity." The 1987 Nicaraguan Constitution recognizes Christian faith in its preamble, describing the country's founders as "those Christians who, inspired by their belief in God, have joined and committed themselves to the struggle for the liberation of the oppressed."

The leader of the Russian Communist Party, Gennady Zyuganov has converted to Orthodox Christianity and accepted Christ. He gives a Christmas message each year. In a 2021 radio interview he said "Put Jesus' Sermon on the Mount and the Moral Code of the Builder of Communism next to each other, and you will just gasp…the main slogan of communism — 'He who does not work shall not eat' — is written in the Apostle Paul's Second Epistle to the Thessalonians…We need to study the Bible."

Hugo Chavez, the founder of the Bolivarian Socialist Republic of Venezuela quoted the Bible in his speeches and was Roman Catholic. His successor, Nicholas Maduro does the same.

Now, none of this matters to you, as you have divorced yourself from all these forces, just as you have divorced yourself from China, Vietnam, Peoples Korea, and the other governments that hold on to the atheistic aspect of Marxism-Leninism. You have even denounced Nepal, where the major Communist party that runs much of the government traces itself back to your ideological brand of "Marxism-Leninism-Maoism" and the Revolutionary Internationalist Movement you helped to form.

Your "anti-revisionism" and ideological purity has rendered you and your "new synthesis" completely cut off from the global communist movement. But this global communist movement that you reject has largely reformed itself on the question of religion. Just as atheism has changed in the 21st century, so has communism.

The atheism of peasants and capitalists trying to overthrow feudalism is very different from the atheism of capitalists insisting that morality is for suckers and that they have been "naturally selected" by evolution to rule over the working class. Religion today is more and more a representation of collectivism, a collectivism that could lay the basis for resistance to capitalist power and imperialism. It is an expression of people refusing to be alienated from each other, and

The revolutionary FSLN government of Nicaragua leads under the slogan "Christianity, Socialism and Solidarity."

joining arm and arm to protect each other from a globalist plutocratic system that is completely Satanic in its essence.

In the past, saying "there is no God' was a way of saying that the world did not have to be as it is. It was a way of defying a power structure that used religion to justify itself. In our time, saying "there is no God" is a way of justifying the ruling order, saying that no true moral or ethical code exists and no spiritual power can be appealed to in order to resist it. Marxism teaches about negation of the negation, and how things become their opposite over time, and this certainly fits the changing role of both religion and atheism in our time.

In your criticism of Christianity, you often point toward Jesus' words that "the last shall be first and the first shall be last." You say that simply reversing the position of oppressors and oppressed is not desirable. Flipping things so one group is oppressed rather than the other is not the goal of the communist revolution, you argue. Christianity and any notion of Christian socialism, you claim, is therefore debunked.

But this is a misunderstanding of Jesus' words. Let us look closely at what Jesus said: "People will come from east and west and north and south, and will take their places at the feast in the kingdom of God. Indeed there are those who are last who will be first, and first who will be last." (Luke 13:29-30) "Anyone who wants to be first must be the very last, and the servant of all." (Mark 9:35) "But many *that are* first shall be last; and the last *shall be* first" (Matthew 19:30) "But many *that are* first shall be last; and the last first." (Mark 10:31)

When Jesus said "the last shall be first and the first shall be last" he was saying something much more profound. In the Book of Revelations, Jesus repeatedly calls himself and is referred to as "The

First and the Last" and "The Alpha and the Omega." "I am the Alpha and the Omega, the First and the Last, the Beginning and the End. "Blessed are those who wash their robes, that they may have the right to the tree of life and may go through the gates into the city." (Revelations 22:13) "Do not be afraid; I am the first and the last, and the living one. I was dead, and see, I am alive forever and ever." (Revelations 1:17-18) This echoes the words of God as quoted by the Prophet Isaiah: "I am the first and I am the last, and apart from me there is no God." (Isaiah 44:6)

It is clear that Jesus is intentionally provoking his followers to rethink their understanding of what "first" and "last" mean. If in order to be "first" one must place themselves as last and be a servant to others (Mark 9:35), what does it even mean? If many who are are first shall be last, and many who are last shall be first, it seems that this order shall be rendered irrelevant by God. And if Jesus is declaring himself to simultaneously be both the first and the last, the alpha and omega, as was said of God by Isaiah, it indicates that such ranking is meaningless.

It appears that with this turn of phrase, repeated throughout the Gospels and New Testament, Jesus is in fact pointing to an aspect of reality that would later become a Hegelian concept called "the unity of opposites." There can be no tall without short. There can be no fast without slow. The concepts rely on each other for their existence.

Furthermore, If Jesus or God, the same entity, is the first and the last, the beginning and the end, then there is no beginning and no end. If the last are first and the first are last, and the way to be first is to make yourself last, then it is pretty clear that any hierarchy or ranking is completely broken down and irrelevant. This is what Christ meant.

Jesus Christ is saying that his mission and the mission of Christianity is to create a world where there are no firsts and lasts. If the last is first and the first is last, if the greatest and least position is occupied by the same entity at the same point in time, there is no hierarchy of any kind. And this is the mission of global communism, to create a world where last and first fade away as concepts. This can be achieved by creating vast abundance so none are without. In essence, Christianity seeks to bring the world into balance. There is no contradiction any longer because all contradictions have been resolved.

I challenge you to read the Christian Gospels, most specifically the words of Jesus Christ himself, and tell me that he was not a heroic revolutionary. He instructs his followers, much as you do, to give the whole of their lives and make great sacrifices for the cause of righteousness, to endure persecution, and to stand with the oppressed while condemning the oppressors.

Christ told his followers that "No one can serve two masters. Either you will hate the one and love the other, or you will be devoted to the one and despise the other. You cannot serve both God and money." (Matthew 6:24) Likewise, the early church said that "the love of money is a root of all kinds of evil." (Timothy 6:10)

When Marx describes communism as "from each according to his own ability, to each according to his need" he was making a biblical allusion. References to distribution according to need can be found in several places in the Bible: "All the believers were one in heart and mind. No one claimed that any of their possessions was their own, but they shared everything they had. With great power the apostles continued to testify to the resurrection of the Lord Jesus. And God's grace was so powerfully at work in them all that there were no needy persons among them. For from time to time those who owned land or houses sold them, brought the money from the sales and put it at the apostles' feet, and it was distributed to anyone who had need." (Acts 4:32-35)

"Everyone was filled with awe at the many wonders and signs performed by the apostles. All the believers were together and had everything in common. They sold property and possessions to give to anyone who had need." (Acts 2:43-44) "Anyone who has been stealing must steal no longer, but must work, doing something useful with their own hands, that they may have something to share with those in need." (Ephesians 4:28)

18. The God I Found

When you toured the country in 1979, rallying support for yourself and the other RCP activists who faced criminal charges for protesting Deng Xiaoping, you often ended your speeches with rant that sounded more or less like this: "Every time we try to change things, they pound their gavel and pull their guns and say: "Overruled!" We go out here every day and what does the ruling class say to us, time and again? "All your hopes and dreams and aspirations for something higher are overruled. All your demands for a better life, your struggling and striving to get out from underneath this, is overruled." With that reactionary message of the imperialist class ringing in our ears, we are going to go out here to work among thousands and millions of people, to move thousands and then through thousands move and influence and organize and channel the hatred of millions. It is going to come to that point where this system is weakened and the determination of the people for change is strengthened and millions of people are going to go from being unarmed - trying to protest or find some peaceful way to change this system by its rules - to saying; "I can't stand this another day, I won't live under it another day. I'm willing to put everything on the line to change it!" At that point our party is going to lead them and organize them in taking up arms with the strength of millions. As we do all this, our vision of the future is going to be before us, and ringing in our ears will be that reactionary message they daily pound into our heads, that everything we hope and strive and struggle for is overruled. As we go and defeat, disintegrate, and win over part of their imperialist army, smash and punish their private reactionary armies; as we shatter and destroy their police forces and punish them for their crimes; as we go in and break the stranglehold of their bureaucracies - break up their administrative hold and apparatus, declaring them null and void - we are going to see those capitalists who have declared everything we want and hope and struggle for overruled. We are

The people of Yemen have withstood an onslaught from US-backed Saudi Arabia, fighting to free their country from the global imperialist system.

going to see them and we are going to chase them into the corner like the reactionary rats they are. As they are in that corner with all their state machinery, their armies, their bureaucracies broken and shattered, and with the conscious force and determination of millions of people rising up in arms, the vision and understanding of their own interests and the future that belongs to them clearly before them - we are going to point those millions of guns squarely at the imperialists, and with their reactionary message ringing in our ears, we are going to look them straight in the eye and say: "Overrule this, Motherfucker!" ("To All Those Who Refuse to Live and Die on Their Knees," Part 2, excerpts from 1979 national speaking tour, RW, No. 243, February 17, 1984, p. 10." Cited in *Bullets*, 1985)

Even though this passage makes no references to religion, I think it accurately summarizes your atheism, as well as the atheism I adopted as a teenager and carried with me up into adulthood. While I have no desire to psychoanalyze you, it is certainly peculiar that you reference the banging of a gavel and "overruled" when your father was a prominent judge.

Regardless, the allegorical judge in this passage is a good stand in for a God which I, like yourself, do not believe in. It presents an all powerful deity who is indifferent to the suffering of humanity. A being that could immediately sweep away all suffering in the world, but chooses not to in order to instead cast moral judgment, and "test" how loyal we are to him as he subjects us to so much misery.

Such a God, who could immediately end all suffering but chooses not to, sees how we react to the pains of this world, and if we react in a faithless or immoral way, or if we choose not bow before his son Jesus Christ, bangs his gavel and casts us into hellfire for eternity. We are told "he loves us." And he "does this for our own good." We are told not to be arrogant and assume we might know better, or try to make logical sense of what he is mercilessly subjecting not just us, but all of humanity too. I stopped believing in this God a long time ago. Like you, I certainly had a desire to "point those millions of guns squarely" at this God, "look them straight in the eye and say: Overrule this, Motherfucker!"

I discovered a new God in 2015, or you could say, I chose to acknowledge him. In 2015 I was on a ship chartered by the Red Crescent Society of the Islamic Republic of Iran headed for war-torn Yemen with medical aid. I feared for my life as Israel and Saudi Arabia both falsely claimed our ship was loaded with weapons, and threatened to attack it.

LETTER TO BOB AVAKIAN

The reason I got on the ship was because I am an anti-imperialist. Saudi Arabia, a brutal US-backed autocracy, armed with US weapons, was waging an all out war against its southern neighbor, Yemen. Yemen had asserted its independence from Saudi domination, and the United States was providing satellite support and weaponry to enable the Saudis reassert control of the country and put their puppet Mansour Hadi back into power. Tens of thousands of Yemenis have died from US bombs dropped by Saudi Arabia, and thousands more died from malnutrition due to the Saudi blockade. As someone living in the center of US imperialism, I felt a need to stand in solidarity with the Yemeni people fighting for their national liberation. I often referred back to the words of Mao Zedong when thinking of the conflict: "A weak nation can defeat a strong, a small nation can defeat a big. The people of a small country can certainly defeat aggression by a big country, if only they dare to rise in struggle, dare to take up arms and grasp in their own hands the destiny of their country. This is a law of history."

Indeed, the people of Yemen, one of the poorest countries in the world, have resisted almost a decade-long onslaught from the country with the fourth largest military budget of any country in the world. The Revolutionary Alliance is fighting for independence, and their logo includes a shaft of wheat which stands for economic development. The Yemenis are fighting, in the name of Islam, to take control of their natural resources and liberate their country from foreign domination and impoverishment as a US/Saudi client state.

I was the only American on the ship, along with a French and German citizen, and a number of Iranians. Less than 10 people onboard were English speakers, and as we spent 13 days on the ocean, we had plenty of time to talk. The Iranians were devout Muslims, hardliners, adherents of the Shia Islamic Revolutionary movement of Imam Khomeni. They questioned me hard about the Bible, the Christian teachings, and my own life, how I had come to be an anti-imperialist.

On the day our ship was set to arrive at the Port of Hodeidah, the Saudis bombed the port 8 times in a single day in order to prevent our medical supplies and food from being delivered. They also bombed and destroyed the medical university in Hodeidah as retaliation for their plan to receive medical supplies from us. I am still haunted by the fact that dock workers and medical students were killed because they wanted to cooperate with me and my Iranian friends in bringing medical aid to the country.

As I sat on this ship in May of 2015, I found out that it was creating an international incident. Reuters and the international press reported heavily on the Iranian Rescue Ship, attempting to break the blockade and deliver food and medical supplies to Yemen. John Kerry was negotiating with Javid Zarif in Vienna, and my name came up in conversations between them. Kerry was angry that they had put some "Occupy Wall Street kid" on the ship, and done so behind his back. I had a sense as I was on the boat, watching the sun set that my life was in danger. I knew that in the Pentagon, in Tel Aviv and in Riyadh there were military analysts calculating a cost benefit analysis of sinking the ship and snuffing out our lives.

As the Iranians kept asking me about the Bible, about Jesus, and about how I, some Irish-American from rural Ohio, had come to risk my life in the Gulf of Aden, I finally could not deny it any longer.

It was the power of God and his son Jesus Christ that compelled me to be on that ship. It was the love for Jesus Christ and his message of kindness, compassion and human brotherhood that I had learned as a small child that had taken me from Ohio to New York City, from New York City to Iran and from Iran to the Gulf of Aden.

I remembered vividly the vacation Bible school I attended each summer at the tiny Lutheran church my grandmother was a member of. The small white building was surrounded entirely by cornfields, with not another building in sight. As a small child I learned about a man who told us to live for the sake of others and set a great example by laying down his life in defiance of the rich and powerful. From the time I was a small child I wanted to live as Jesus had lived, I wanted to be revolutionary and a fighter for justice who was strong enough to endure the harshest persecution and suffering in order to bring some kindness into this cruel and unjust world.

God was not something that had to be proven to me. God was something I could feel. God was all around me. God was an energy, a source of power and connection between human beings. God was an inner strength, a source of power that can be found in every corner of the universe compelling us to resist Satan.

And no, this God is not a patriarchal all-powerful deity. This God is an energy, a strength, a life force, a creative power. I had felt this God in Ecuador among Communist activists from across the planet who gathered for the World Festival of Youth and Students. I had felt this God among the Black people who pulled together against police brutality in Cleveland. I had felt this God thinking of so many people who have given their lives to the struggle for justice, not for any reward they might receive in this life, but for the truth and goodness they felt deeply within. I am forced think of how the writer Anna Louise Strong, who was a friend of Stalin and Mao, wrote of how much of her accomplishments in life was motivated by a desire to feel she was "right in her soul."

This God is within all of us, whether we choose to hear it or not. However, when we combine together and support each other, when we step out of our individualism this God's power compounds and multiplies. This is why Jesus told his followers "For where two or three gather in my name, there am I with them." (Matthew 18:20) God is not all powerful, and he does not control this world. This world is ruled by Satan and the forces of darkness, but it is our duty as revolutionaries to conquer it for God, to complete Jesus' mission and bring back Eden, to construct God's Kingdom on Earth.

It was in the Gulf of Aden that I surrendered myself to this God. I gave Him full control over me and my future. I accepted that even if I must die, and even if I must be completely forgotten, I will have lived best by glorifying Him and giving myself to His truths.

Years later I would read about how Sigmund Freud was perplexed by how his patients described their connection to God, writing: "It is a feeling which he would like to call a sensation of 'eternity', a feeling as of something limitless and unbounded - as it were, oceanic. This feeling, he adds, is a purely subjective fact, not an article of faith; it brings with it no assurance of personal immortality, but a source of religious energy seized upon by various churches and religious systems, directed by them into particular channels, and doubtless exhausted by them. One may, he thinks, rightly call oneself religious on the grounds of this

LETTER TO BOB AVAKIAN

oceanic feeling even if one rejects every faith and every illusion."

And while you may laugh at me, I would contend that it is this beautiful oceanic sensation of eternity that has driven every great revolutionary movement. It was God who compelled the Soviet people to fight so heroically against the Nazis. It was God that enabled Mao to build his peasant army and mobilize millions to fight for a new China. It was God that pushed Che Guevara to give up his life of privilege and become a guerrilla fighter for the people.

I would argue that one of the primary aims of the imperialists in our time is to try and stamp out these feelings of solidarity, these feelings of revolutionary passion, wherever they exist. With their endless Netflix documentaries warning about "cults," and their constant trafficking in cynicism, sarcasm and pessimism, they hope to prevent any form of spiritual collective power from emerging among us.

I think about Stalin, the leader of the Soviet Union, and how you often reference that he was trained in a seminary school. Simon Sebag Montifore, the right-wing British historian, also notes this when analyzing Stalin. Unlike you, Montifore sees this as a source of Stalin's strength as an organizer. In his biography *Young Stalin* he writes about how: "The workers listened reverently to this young preacher — and it was no coincidence that many of the revolutionaries were seminarists, and the workers often pious ex-peasants... Trotsky, agitating in another city, remembered that many of the workers thought the movement resembled the early Christians and had to be taught that they should be atheists."

Stalin brought back the Russian Orthodox Church during the Second World War. As the country faced the onslaught of a Nazi invasion, the cathedrals were reopened and Russians said the same ancient prayers they had recited for centuries. The state remained atheistic and materialist, but Sergei Eisenstein's film *Ivan the Terrible* contained many scenes of Christian prayer and worship.

It is because of his role in defeating Nazis and his decision to promote religion and re-legalize the Church during the Second World War that one can find images of Stalin inside many Orthodox Churches in Russia today. Polls show that Stalin is overwhelmingly popular among the Russian people, even among those who consider themselves not to be Communists. Stalin is more popular than Lenin, and many Orthodox religious believers maintain that he was one of them despite his many public statements to the contrary.

And let it be noted that one event that set the stage for the fall of the USSR was Khruschev's secret speech of 1956. When Khruschev got up before the 20th Party Congress of the Communist Party of the Soviet Union and unloaded a mostly fictional tirade against Stalin, it devastated the Soviet people. Stalin had been the leader who mobilized the country to build and construct. Stalin had led them through the Second World War and then the reconstruction of the country afterward. Stalin had overseen the mobilization of the population to raise the country up from nothing and industrialize with collective effort. The Soviet people had seen 27 million of their countryfolk die but yet had found the strength to get through it all and emerge victorious. Stalin had been the man at the center of all of it, motivating people, rewarding high achievers with the Stakhanovite movement, and playing the role of the spiritual father for millions.

Stalin's ability to motivate the population to build had not been merely rational or materialistic, it had a spiritual quality. Demonizing him and besmirching his reputation had psychologically raped the Soviet people. It had created an atmosphere of cynicism and hopelessness.

This is why the imperialists celebrated the Secret Speech, and this is why the imperialists are working to abolish religion, ideology and mass movements of any kind in our time. They see this spiritual power as a threat. They seek to destroy it as it is the only thing that can stand in their way, and truly is the only thing that ever has.

As I reflected on earlier, while you claim to be a true materialist, I see spirituality all over your work. Your analysis of socialist countries and why they should be supported or opposed, your gut level opposition to Trump when his faction is disfavored by the imperialists, your ability to mobilize people and work them up into a frenzy to achieve organizational goals, all of this has a spiritual quality. There are religious feelings and a desire for spiritual euphoria all over your movement and all across your work.

By denying it, and pretending your work is purely materialist, you have allowed these feelings and spiritual aspirations to be uncontrolled. Economic analysis should not be influenced by how you feel, or whether or not a society gives you vibes of liberation. Understanding of world events and which factions in the ruling class to strategically align with should not be motivated by how Donald Trump makes you feel or the vibe he gives you.

Religious and spiritual feelings are vitally important in building an organization and holding a group of people together. However, they should not calculate into analysis of the economy, utilizing scientific Marxism to calculate the nature of reality and the trajectory of the world.

Part of the reason our movement has suffered so many losses since the end of the Second World War has been our unhealthy relationship with the spiritual aspect of humanity. The imperialists have launched very effective psychological operations against socialist countries, and socialist movements have been significantly weakened in their ability to maintain the trust of the masses because of this oversight.

Human beings are spiritual in nature, and they are not merely another animal. They have a unique, creative power that separates them from the animal kingdom. As Engels noted: "the animal merely *uses* its environment, and brings about changes in it simply by its presence; man by his changes makes it serve his ends, *masters* it. This is the final, essential distinction between man and other animals."

The resurgent socialist and anti-imperialist bloc of today seems to have acknowledged this to a significant degree, and is utilizing it to rebuild what has been lost. The fact that the revolutionary forces remain in power in Venezuela, despite everything that country has been subjected to since the death of Hugo Chavez is a tremendous testament to the strength of Maduro and the revolutionary movement there. I greatly doubt that they would have such strength if they embraced cold materialism and atheism. What I saw in Central Caracas in 2015 in the collectives and communes was thousands of dark-skinned working class Venezuelans, who believed in God with every ounce of their being, and saw God's mission on earth as fulfilled with resistance to capitalism and the construction of 21st Century Socialism.

19. "Where Does This Revolution Come From?"

As I conclude this letter, I must say I am nervous about publishing it. One of my frustrations with your organization over the years has been that you have this great desire for people to "engage with Bob Avakian's work," however, your response to criticism of it is often not positive. If a review summarizes your work, even with a positive assessment, you often take issue with it being not a correct summary and your supporters lash out. Furthermore, if a review criticizes your work as I have just done, you may consider it harsh slander or the work of the enemy.

I am not your enemy. For all the good you have done over the course of your life, I salute you. You are a big reason that Mumia Abu Jamal is still alive. You were a major factor in opposing the US invasion of Iraq, protecting civil liberties and free speech over the course of decades, and showing the American people very loudly that Communism as a movement was and is alive and well in our country.

I'm only 35 years old, and I have been organizing the Center for Political Innovation for just a few years. I have been subjected already to just a fraction of the personal attacks, smearing, government intimidation you have faced. I must admit that when I was a younger man, before I had the experiences I have now had, I was guilty of spreading gossip and rumors about you, speaking of you in negative and unfair terms, and otherwise disrespecting you in an unprincipled and dishonest way.

For that I sincerely apologize.

In this letter, I have tried to be as intellectually honest and fair as possible. I have tried to back up everything I have said with evidence and every statement attributed to you with an actual quotation. I do not think you will change your mind, and I have not written this with such intentions. This is a public document for me to use your views and statements and contrast them with my own perspective. This is a polemic, a staple of the Marxist tradition, along the lines of *Anti-Duhring*, *The Poverty of Philosophy*, *The Critique of the Gotha Program*, *Left-Wing Communism* and similar works.

If you or your organization takes great offense to what I have written, or finds it highly objectionable, or if you find it to be an honest contrasting of world views, I would be deeply honored to see a response in print. It would be the highest level compliment to have this text acknowledged by yourself and your organization. I honestly doubt that you will respond to what is written above, but it would be deeply appreciated and would contribute to the kind of lively atmosphere of debate and discussion that your New Synthesis claims to promote.

I can assure you that this piece is not the work of some kind of COINTELPRO-style operation, and is not intended to stir up more controversy or drama. I wrote this work hoping that the audience would come away from it with an accurate assessment of our very different interpretations of the same overall worldview, the struggle to build a stateless, classless world without inequality, the great project of communism.

I want to end with one final point. Years ago, when I was getting involved in the Workers World Party, I showed your DVD *Revolution: Why It's Necessary, Why It's Possible, What It's All About* to an elderly comrade. This woman had parents who had been in the Communist Party USA during the

1930s. She had attended young pioneer summer camps and grown up in Brooklyn. She had been a founding member of the Workers World Party, having been in Sam Marcy's faction of the Socialist Workers Party prior to that.

She watched you begin by singing Bob Dylan's lyrics about "selling postcards of the hanging…" and go on to describe the ugliness of lynching, and then compare it to the horrific details of police brutality, and then from there emphasize that revolution is the solution. After watching you speak for several hours she gave me her criticism as a long-time communist. She said "He's only telling half the story."

She asked why you did not tell of John Brown's raid on Harper's Ferry or Nat Turner's slave revolt. She asked why you did not speak of the Deacons for Defense or the African Blood Brotherhood, or the interracial sharecroppers unions the

Communist Party built throughout the Jim Crow south, bringing Black and white workers together to oppose the capitalist system.

"Where does he think this revolution is going to come from?" She asked. This moment was a huge one in my political education which I often refer back to years later. To this woman who had spent her life in the Communist movement from her childhood in the 1930s up to her death in 2014, you came across as a Utopian socialist. You did not place your revolution in the context of the working class movement, the anti-racist struggles, and the anti-war protests of the past. You did not insert yourself into the ongoing battles taking place in US society, and present socialism and revolution as the victory of all the progressive forces that have existed before. You presented socialism and communism almost like they were a magical formula that you came into town selling one day, to solve all problems.

In doing so, you write yourself out of American history. You almost surrender the entire context of US society to other forces. Karl Marx did not do this when Lincoln battled the slaveholders. Marx understood that in order for the Communist movement to be relevant, it had to attach itself to the progressive struggle of the abolitionists, the slave revolutionaries, the labor movement and even the industrial capitalists in their efforts to defeat the slaveholders in the South. Joseph Weydmeyer and August Willich became important leaders of the Union Army. Marx wrote for the *New York Tribune*, the Republican Party aligned newspaper of New York City, edited by Horace Greely. The International Workingmen's Association organized workers in Britain to hold mass rallies supporting Lincoln, and to refuse to work with cotton imported from the United States, picked by slaves.

If you understand it is necessary to attach yourself to certain forces and make strategic alliances in divisions in the ruling class, why does it not follow that you should present your movement as a continuation and concentration of progressive strands and forces of resistance that already exist in US society? Marxism does not teach that the revolution comes from thin air, but that it comes from material contradictions and existing social forces. Why is attaching your organization and its legacy to those forces not part of how you present communism? Why does your communism seem to be an alien, disconnected force, a kind of magical solution?

The revolution I want to build is a continuation of the progressive struggles that have taken place on this soil for hundreds of years. It is the culmination of the labor movement, the struggle for peace, the struggle for equal rights and liberty. It is the construction of an anti-monopoly coalition to defeat the imperialists and rebuild the United States as a society where the banks, factories and centers of economic power work in the interests of society overall, not for the profits of a wealthy few.

I will never forget the day when I was 15 years-old that I got to spend the afternoon at a bookstore run by your cadre. My mother told me not to leave the store under any circumstances. But after our discussion of Bush ended, the comrades said it was time to go out and sell the paper. They handed me a stack of newspapers.

I looked on in horror, thinking "You have got to be kidding me." The idea of walking up to strangers, people I did not know, and trying to get them to pay me actual money for a newspaper about communism seemed outrageous. I was shy. I was nervous. But the comrades said "Come on, we do it all the time."

I went out onto the streets of the Coventry neighborhood in Cleveland Heights, Ohio, and I sold communist newspapers.

That day saved my life. It was my first step out of the shell of isolation and depression I had trapped myself in. It was my first step toward discovering my own identity and breaking away from the roles and labels my family had placed on me. It was my first step toward having real friends and knowing what it meant to be part of a real group of dedicated people struggling for a cause.

That day I joined a movement. I had said I believed in communism before that. I had argued about it on the internet and debated people in my school, but I had never really done anything about it. For too many young people I meet now, Communism is just an internet hobby, or a commodified identity as my friend, filmmaker Peter Coffin describes it. Communism is a way to complain about the world and put a label on yourself. Communism is a fantasy for people who feel alienated from the society they live in.

But the day I first sold your newspaper with a team of young cadres, I joined a movement. That was the day I started to have self-esteem and be proud of who I was as a Communist. That was the day I began to perfect my ability to interact with people, that was a pivotal day in the history of my life. That was the day I took my first steps toward New York City, Iran, Russia, and Venezuela. That was the day the person I have become today, as much as you may disapprove, was born.

For this I am eternally grateful to you. It has taken me years to realize what you did for me. It has also taken me years to see that my generation and the generations younger than me are full of young people who have the same hopelessness, the same pessimism, the same lack of self-esteem and lack of self-empowerment that I had. Millions of young Americans desperately need a movement, just like I did.

I intend to give it to them. I intend to save their lives, just as you saved mine. I intend to keep the flame of revolution burning, even if I understand it far differently than you do.

With sincerity and honesty,

Caleb T. Maupin,
Ideological Leader of the Center for Political Innovation

The Center for Political Innovation continues to hold rallies around the country, working to build a community of anti-imperialists.

LETTER TO BOB AVAKIAN